T0001233

TOP **10**
SINGAPORE

Top 10 Singapore Highlights

The Top 10 of Everything

CONTENTS

Singapore Area by Area

Streetsmart

Within each Top 10 list in this book, no hierarchy of quality or popularity is implied. All 10 are, in the editor's opinion, of roughly equal merit.
  Throughout this book, floors are referred to in accordance with American usage; i.e., the "first floor" is at ground level.

Title page, front cover and spine *The stunning Supertree Grove at the Gardens by the Bay park in Marina Bay*
Back cover, clockwise from top left *Detail of Sri Mariamman Temple; Singapore skyline at night; Pedestrians in Chinatown; Supertree Grove; Interior of Marina Bay Sands*

The rapid rate at which the world is changing is constantly keeping the DK Eyewitness team on our toes. While we've worked hard to ensure that this edition of Singapore is accurate and up-to-date, we know that opening hours alter, standards shift, prices fluctuate, places close and new ones pop up in their stead. So, if you notice we've got something wrong or left something out, we want to hear about it. Please get in touch at **travelguides@dk.com**

Welcome to
Singapore

Lion city. Major Asian powerhouse. Cultural melting pot. Shopping mecca. Fusion-food heaven. An island city-state of gleaming skyscrapers and primary rainforest, the Republic of Singapore contrasts striking modernity with its traditional heritage like nowhere else. With DK Eyewitness Top 10 Singapore, it's yours to explore.

Small and densely populated, this tropical city-state is constantly reinventing itself. The space-age **Gardens by the Bay**, part natural wonder, part epic fantasy land, face the downtown urban jungle. While looking to the future, Singapore embraces its past. Its colonial legacy is preserved in Palladian buildings housing the **National Gallery** and the **Asian Civilisation Museum**. Poignant memories of **World War II** are scattered across the island, while pre-war shophouses have been reborn as hip boutiques and cafés.

Singapore is full of surprises: Taoist and Hindu temples, Muslim mosques, and Christian churches share streets with sublime spas and chic rooftop bars. Whether you are eyeing designer goods in the luxury malls of **Orchard Road**, weaving through stalls in **Chinatown**, sipping a Singapore Sling in **Raffles Hotel**, or slurping a fiery laksa in an open-air hawker center, there is never enough time for everything on offer. With eye-catching festivals and events, from **Chinese New Year** to the Singapore Grand Prix, it's all here.

Whether you're visiting for a weekend or a week, our Top 10 guide brings together the best of everything Singapore has to offer, from the bright lights of **Marina Bay** to the boisterous laneways of **Little India**. The guide has useful tips throughout, from seeking out what's free to avoiding the crowds, plus seven easy-to-follow itineraries, designed to tie together a clutch of sights in a short space of time. Add inspiring photography and detailed maps, and you've got the essential pocket-sized travel companion. **Enjoy the book, and enjoy Singapore.**

Clockwise from top: Thian Hock Keng Temple, ION Orchard mall, Gardens by the Bay, the Marina Bay skyline, Chinese New Year celebrations, Raffles Hotel, Fort Canning Park

Exploring Singapore

For sights to see and cultures to experience, visitors to Singapore are spoiled for choice. Whether you have a couple of days' stopover between flights or have come to get a fuller flavor of this city-state, here are some ideas for two and four days of sightseeing in Singapore.

Orchard Road is lined with a number of luxury malls, such as Paragon

Two Days in Singapore

Day ❶

MORNING

Start with a grand breakfast at **Raffles Hotel** *(see pp30–31)* before visiting the **National Museum of Singapore** *(see pp12–13)* for an hour or two. Take in luxury malls on **Orchard Road** *(see pp94–9)* or check out the **Singapore Botanic Gardens** *(see pp24–5)*.

AFTERNOON

Immerse yourself in Chinatown, visit **Thian Hock Keng Temple** *(see pp16–17)*, then stroll (or take a bumboat) along the **Singapore River** *(see pp14–15)*. Finish your river tour with a sunset drink atop **Marina Bay Sands** *(see p26)* and circle the lit-up bay at night.

Day ❷

MORNING

Begin by exploring the colorful lanes of **Little India and Kampong Glam** *(see pp78–85)*. Admire the

Key

— Two-day itinerary
— Four-day itinerary

Sri Veeramakaliamman Temple *(see pp20–21)* and **Sultan Mosque** *(see pp18–19)*, and try local food in a hawker center *(see pp60–61)*.

AFTERNOON

Depending on your interests, head to the beaches and attractions on **Sentosa** island *(see pp32–3)* or spend the afternoon at the vast **Gardens by the Bay** *(see pp28–9)*, winding up with dinner at the open-air food court, **Satay by the Bay**.

Sentosa Island provides a tranquil getaway from the bustle of the city

Clarke Quay is a great spot for a riverside evening drink

Day ❷
MORNING
Check out the Civic District's architecture, potter around **Raffles Hotel** (see pp30–31) and browse Southeast Asian masterpieces in the **National Gallery Singapore** (see p40).
AFTERNOON
Dip into **Katong/Joo Chiat** (see p104) for Peranakan food and architecture, before shopping in Bugis or along Raffles Boulevard. After a "flight" on the **Singapore Flyer**, close out the day at **Marina Bay** (see pp26–7).

Day ❸
MORNING
Begin early to enjoy either fun-filled **Sentosa** (see pp32–3) or a trip to **Pulau Ubin** (see p103) to experience old rural Singapore.
AFTERNOON
Take a stroll along the stunning **Southern Ridges** (see p100) before hitting charming **Dempsey Hill** (see p104) for dinner and cocktails.

Day ❹
MORNING
Start off with a morning turn in **Kampong Glam** for boutiques and brunch, then explore **Little India**'s Hindu temples (see pp78–81). Hit up the malls on **Orchard Road** (see pp94–9), finishing at the **National Orchid Garden** in the **Singapore Botanic Gardens** (see pp24–5).
AFTERNOON
Head down to **Gardens by the Bay** (see pp28–9) and spend an afternoon cooling down in the domed Cloud Forest. Come evening, return east to catch a live show at **Marina Bay Sands** (see p26) or **Esplanade – Theatres on the Bay** (see p64).

Sri Mariamman Temple, Singapore's oldest Hindu place of worship

---

Four Days in Singapore

Day ❶
MORNING
Visit **Thian Hock Keng Temple** (see pp16–17) and Chinatown's shops (see p76). Next, head to the **National Museum of Singapore** (see pp12–13).
AFTERNOON
Head across the road to **Fort Canning Park** (see p90). Look out for the shrine of Iskandar Shah, ruler of ancient Singapura, and visit Battlebox, a World War II underground bunker. End the day with drinks at **Clarke Quay** (see p15).

Top 10 Singapore Highlights

The otherworldly Supertree Grove at Gardens by the Bay

TOP 10 Singapore Highlights

At the crossroads of east and west, Singapore has a complex mix of culture and history. The Neo-Classical buildings of the Civic District stand alongside the lively neighborhoods of Chinatown, Little India, and Kampong Glam, with the Singapore River carving its way between them. It is a multifaceted city with both traditional and modern appeal.

National Museum of Singapore ①

The ideal introduction to Singapore and its cultural influences, the refurbished museum presents history using multimedia displays *(see pp12–13)*.

Singapore River ②

The Singapore River is lined by dining and leisure establishments. It is best experienced aboard a restored bumboat *(see pp14–15)*.

Thian Hock Keng Temple ③

This is Singapore's first Chinese Taoist temple and one of its finest. It is a good starting point for exploring Chinatown *(see pp16–18)*.

Sultan Mosque ④

With its gold onion domes that rise above Kampong Glam, the city's traditional Muslim quarter, Sultan Mosque is a fine blend of Persian, Moorish, and Turkish design *(see pp18–19)*.

Sri Veeramakaliamman Temple ⑤

Statues of Hindu gods crowd this temple's roof, watching over Little India. Dedicated to the goddess Kali, this temple is one of Singapore's oldest *(see pp20–21)*.

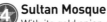

LITTLE INDIA ⑤

PRINSEP ST
BENCOOLEN ST
ROCHOR
JALAN BESAR
VICTORIA ST
N BRIDGE
BRAS BASAH RD

Fort Canning Park

① ⑨

STAMFORD RD

RIVER VALLEY RD

B BRIDGE RD

Padang

②

NEW BRIDGE RD
N CANAL RD
SOUTH BRIDGE
CHURCH ST
CROSS ST
COLLYER QUAY

CHINATOWN ST
③
RAFFLES QUAY
MAXWELL RD

MARINA BAY

0 meters 800
0 yards 800

Singapore Botanic Gardens ⑥

On sprawling grounds just beyond the city center, the beautifully maintained Singapore Botanic Gardens are especially refreshing in the early mornings, when the air is a little cooler *(see pp24–5)*.

⑦ Marina Bay

Surrounded by iconic Singapore sights such as the Merlion, Marina Bay Sands, and the impressive Singapore Flyer, the bay's skyline is breathtaking both day and night *(see pp26–7)*.

⑧ Gardens by the Bay

This green development has futuristic biodomes, solar-powered "supertrees", and sculptures by some of the world's leading contemporary artists *(see pp28–9)*.

⑨ Raffles Hotel

Renowned writers, including Joseph Conrad and Somerset Maugham, stayed at this luxurious hotel in its early 20th-century heyday. This is the place where the famous Singapore Sling cocktail was invented *(see pp30–31)*.

Sentosa ⑩

Singapore's popular playground, Sentosa is an island of relaxing spas and resorts, thrilling water and land sports, and other attractions *(see pp32–3)*.

TOP10 ⭐ National Museum of Singapore

Dedicated to Singapore's fascinating history and culture, the National Museum of Singapore was established in the late 1800s and is the oldest museum in the country. It is housed in a large classical building designed in Neo-Palladian and Renaissance style. Behind the building is a glass and steel modern wing, which offers a striking contrast to the original structure. The museum features multimedia exhibits that bring the story of Singapore to life.

4 The Glass Passage

The construction of the glass passage is an architectural achievement and a visually stunning link between old and new.

5 Surviving Syonan

Visit an exhibition that looks at the ways the local people responded to the harsh conditions of Japanese occupation, when the island was renamed Syonan-to.

1 Architecture and Design

The museum was built to Sir Henry McCallum and John McNair's design in 1887. The Neo-Palladian architecture **(above)** was joined in 2006 by a stunning Modernist structure by local W Architects that more than doubled the size of the building.

2 Singapore History Gallery

Displaying coins, jewelry, ceramics, and more, this gallery covers all of Singapore's history up to modern times. A spiral path leads to a fragment of the Singapore Stone *(see p15)* and the Revere Bell **(right)**.

3 Modern Colony Gallery

This gallery explores the cosmopolitan nature of the city and the lives of wealthy residents during the 1920s and 1930s **(left)**. There is a focus on the role of women in what was for them a time of progressive education and increasingly visible public life.

6 Life in Singapore: The Past 100 Years

The four permanent galleries on Level 2 of the old wing are the Surviving Syonan, Modern Colony, Growing Up, and Voices of Singapore galleries, which present snapshots of everyday life through different eras of Singapore's history.

8 Growing Up Gallery

The 1950s and 1960s were a turbulent period. Growing Up **(left)** shows how post-war children grew up amid social upheaval, and explores how villages, schools, and entertainment venues helped them to evolve a sense of self.

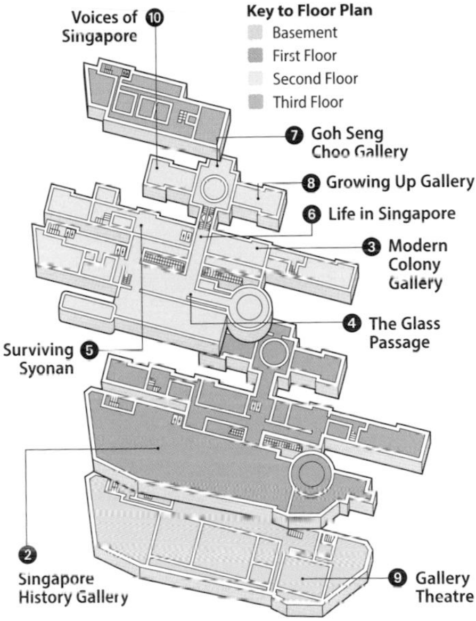

THE ROTUNDA DOME

The National Museum's most iconic architectural feature is the Rotunda Dome. In 2003, extensive restoration work was carried out on the dome's fish-scale zinc tiles and stained glass panels, when they were removed, cleaned and repaired. The final effect is stunning. On a clear day, the sun filtering through the Victorian floral and square patterns throws a ring of pretty colored lights on the floor.

Key to Floor Plan
- Basement
- First Floor
- Second Floor
- Third Floor

Voices of Singapore ⑩

⑦ Goh Seng Choo Gallery

⑧ Growing Up Gallery

⑥ Life in Singapore

❸ Modern Colony Gallery

❹ The Glass Passage

Surviving Syonan ❺

❷ Singapore History Gallery

⑨ Gallery Theatre

National Museum of Singapore

9 Gallery Theatre

The museum holds regular film screenings, talks and other events in its 247-seat theater.

10 Voices of Singapore

Focusing on the 1970s and 1980s, this gallery **(below)** explores how locals formed a distinct national identity while maintaining their varied cultural roots.

7 Goh Seng Choo Gallery

This holds a selection of botanical illustrations from the William Farquhar Collection of Natural History Drawings. Watercolor studies of regional flora are enriched by "scent stations," featuring some of the plants.

NEED TO KNOW

MAP L1 ■ 93 Stamford Rd ■ 6332-3659 ■ www. nhb.gov.sg

Open 10am–7pm daily; last admission to the Glass Rotunda at 6:15pm; other galleries at 6:30pm

Adm S$15 adults, S$10 children, students, and senior citizens; free for under-6s

■ The museum has a café and a modern European restaurant on the first floor, Flutes.

■ The National Museum offers access facilities to those with specific needs.

TOP 10 ★ Singapore River

Flowing past the 1920s godowns (warehouses), the bars and restaurants of Clarke Quay, and the skyscrapers of the financial district, the Singapore River has always been at the center of city life. The river was the first thing to attract Sir Thomas Stamford Raffles, considered the founder of modern Singapore, and a walk along the banks still offers some of the city's most iconic views. Better still, step aboard one of the bumboats that once jostled for space around Boat Quay. Since an intensive clean-up operation in 1987, the river has become a hub of activity, day and night. It may no longer be the main artery of commerce, but it has moved on from its polluted past.

1 Riverboat Trips

Old-fashioned bumboats take around 40 minutes to cruise along the river, past the quays and across Marina Bay. Payment is via booths by the riverside. Tourist boats provide tour commentary through a pre-recorded tape.

3 Asian Civilisations Museum

Built in 1867, these riverfront former government offices were reopened as the Asian Civilisations Museum (see p41) in 2003 (left).

4 Elgin Bridge

The oldest river crossing point was but a wooden drawbridge in 1822. The current bridge, completed in 1929, is named after the Earl of Elgin, Governor General of India in the 1960s.

2 Boat Quay

The quay hasn't stopped buzzing since Chinese merchants first built their godowns here in 1820. Most of the boats have gone, and the quay is now lined with bars and restaurants.

NEED TO KNOW

Asian Civilisations Museum:
MAP M3; 1 Empress Place; 6332-7798; open 10am–7pm Sun–Thu, 10am–9pm Fri; adm S$20 adults, S$15 students and senior citizens; free for under-6s; www.acm.org.sg

Old Parliament House:
MAP M3; 1 Old Parliament Lane; 6332-6900; open 10am–9pm daily; adm for events; www.theartshouse.sg

■ Take a Singapore River Cruise (see p109) boat trip to appreciate the skyline.

5 Clarke Quay

Singapore's favorite evening spot, Clarke Quay is the river's largest conservation project **(below)**. Godowns have been renovated to create a fashionable hub of waterfront bars and restaurants.

Singapore River

656 yards (600 meters)

325 yards (300 meters)

Clarke Quay

HILL ST
N. BRIDGE ROAD
Singapore River
S BRIDGE RD
NORTH CANAL RD
BATTERY ROAD
COLLYER QUAY

8 Alkaff Bridge

Unmissable even from afar, this vibrantly colored footbridge was painted by Filipino artist Pacita Abad. Its shape evokes that of a *tongkang*, a traditional light boat once used to transport goods along the river.

9 Cavenagh Bridge

Designed as a drawbridge and built in Glasgow, this bridge was named after a former governor. Long since pedestrianized, it has a Victorian sign forbidding the passage of livestock.

THE SINGAPORE STONE

On display in the National Museum *(see pp12–13)*, this fragment of inscribed sandstone remains a mystery. Part of a rock discovered at the mouth of the river in 1819, its 50 lines of inscription eluded translation by scholars. The rock was blown up in 1843 on the orders of a British engineer. This piece is one of at least three surviving relics.

6 Robertson Quay

As trade thrived, the swampland upriver was reclaimed and used to build godowns, creating Robertson Quay. The redeveloped area is now a popular metropolitan waterfront scene, lined with chic restaurants, bars, and galleries.

7 Old Parliament House

Singapore's oldest building **(below)**, erected in 1827, once housed the Parliament *(see p42)*, and is now an arts venue, the Arts House.

10 People of the River Sculpture Series

At various points along the river, four bronze sculptures by four Asian artists depict scenes from early Singapore, featuring laborers, merchants **(above)**, and carefree children about to jump into the water.

TOP 10 ⭐ Thian Hock Keng Temple

Built in 1839, this is the oldest Chinese temple in Singapore. It was raised by sailors in homage to the goddess Ma Zu, who, it is believed, laid down her life to give seafarers a safe passage. The temple, paid for by individual donors such as Hokkien leader Tan Tock Seng, was constructed without the use of nails in the southern Chinese architectural style. It is laid out along a traditional north-south axis, with shrines to several deities.

1 Door Paintings
Paintings on the door depict auspicious creatures **(left)**. In Taoist tradition, these protect the temple. A plank across the threshold keeps ghosts away, and ensures visitors bow heads upon entering.

2 Construction
Craftsmen from Southern China built the temple in the traditional manner using no nails. All of the building materials were imported from China, including ironwood for the pillars and pottery used in the roof's mosaics.

NEED TO KNOW
MAP L4 ■ 158 Telok Ayer St ■ 6423-4616 ■ www.thianhockkeng.com.sg

Open 7:30am–5:30pm daily

■ Thian Hock Keng celebrates festivals such as the Chinese Lunar New Year and the birthdays of Guan Yin and Ma Zu with prayer, traditional music, and dance. Since all Chinese holidays are guided by the lunar calendar, it is best to ask the temple exactly when these holidays fall.

■ At the corner of Telok Ayer and Amoy streets, a popular hawker center offers drinks, local dishes, and fruit.

3 The Front Step
The temple was originally located on the seafront, but extensive land reclamation has since cut it off from the coast. The raised step protected it from the high tides that once lapped at its foundations.

4 The Ceiling
During the renovation of the temple in 2000, artists from China were brought in to restore the carvings on the ceiling under the main altar, and to return the gold leaf and bright paintwork to their original splendor.

5 Guan Yin, the Goddess of Mercy
In the courtyard behind the main altar sits Guan Yin **(below)**, the Goddess of Mercy. She is said to have rejected nirvana to return to earth especially to help the needy and those less fortunate.

8 Ancestral Tablets

In keeping with the Taoist practice of ancestor worship, ancestral tablets **(left)** inscribed with the names and dates of departed devotees, are regularly tended with offerings of incense, food, and prayers.

ETIQUETTE IN CHINESE TEMPLES

As in any place of worship, respect for devotees deep in prayer is appreciated. Taking photos is permitted, but visitors must refrain from touching anything on altars. Unlike in Hindu temples or Muslim mosques, clothing norms here are relaxed. Shorts and sleeveless tops are allowed, and footwear can be worn inside the temple.

Thian Hock Keng Temple

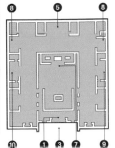

6 Chong Hock Girls' School

Next door to the temple, shops occupy the site of one of Singapore's first girls' schools **(above)**. It was funded by the Huay Kuan, a Hokkien clan association; it and similar groups were the backbone of the local Chinese.

7 Ma Zu, the Guardian of the South Seas

The main hall contains an image of Ma Zu, said to have been born in AD 960 in China's southern Fujian province. Having risked her life to save seafarers, she is worshipped as a goddess.

9 Statue of Confucius

Confucius **(below)**, one of China's greatest thinkers (551–479 BC), developed a social value system that promoted self-discipline, respect for family, education, and political responsibility – values that continue to shape Chinese society today.

10 Statue of Kai Zhang Sheng Wang

This Chinese governor was so successful in developing the economy and improving living standards for the poor that the Hokkien people came to worship him as a deity.

ᴛᴏᴘ10 ⭐ Sultan Mosque

The Sultan Mosque is located in the neighborhood that, in 1819, was assigned to the Malay Sultan of Johor who ruled Singapore. The original mosque that stood on this site was constructed in 1824. Partially funded by the East India Company, it was the style of mosque typically found in Southeast Asia, with a low, two-tiered roof like a pyramid. A century later, the old mosque had fallen into a state of disrepair and was replaced. Swan & Maclaren, the local architects responsible for many landmark buildings, designed it.

4 The Bottle Band
Around the base of the main onion dome is a wide, black band made from glass bottle ends. The bottles were donated by poor members of the community following an initiative to include all Muslims, not just the rich, to contribute to the rebuilding of the mosque.

1 The Central Prayer Hall
Large enough to fit 5,000 devotees, the main hall **(above)** is for men only, while women occupy the galleries above. The carpet, donated by a Saudi Arabian prince, bears his emblem.

2 The Mihrab
The *mihrab* is a small niche that marks the direction of Mecca, and it is from where the imam leads the congregation in prayer five times a day. This altar is decorated with intricately patterned gold motifs.

3 The Mimbar
On Fridays, which is the Muslim holy day, the imam delivers his sermon, or *khutba*, to a full prayer hall. He does so from the *mimbar* **(right)**, an elaborate pulpit atop a staircase reserved for the purpose.

NEED TO KNOW
MAP H5 ▪ 3 Muscat St ▪ 6293-4405
▪ www.sultanmosque.sg

Open 10am–noon & 2–4pm Sat–Thu (from 2:30pm Fri)

▪ During Ramadan, the month of fasting, the streets around the mosque fill with stalls and stores selling delicious Malay treats mid-afternoon onward.

▪ Sip Turkish or Malay-style tea or fresh lime juice in the cafés along Bussorah Street, opposite the mosque.

Sultan Mosque

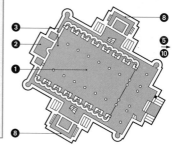

9 Architectural Design
The mosque is built in Saracenic style **(left)**, combining Persian, Moorish, and Turkish design including pointed arches, minarets, and domes. The interior is adorned with calligraphic verses and mosaics.

10 The Annex
Mosques serve many purposes for Muslims – providing space for education, religious rituals, and community development programs. The annex at the Sultan Mosque, built in 1993, offers these services to the local Muslim community.

5 The Maqam
At the rear of the mosque is a *makam*, or mausoleum, containing the graves of several members of the Royal Family, including the grandson of Sultan Hussein Shah, who signed over Singapore to Sir Stamford Raffles in 1819.

6 Mosque Alignment
Most mosques are built with the prayer hall facing the holy city of Mecca. For this reason, North Bridge Road has a distinct bend to allow for the correct alignment of Sultan Mosque.

7 The Domes
A tradition in mosque architecture, the onion dome originates from Turkey and the Middle East. It creates a roofline distinguishable above the city's low-rise buildings. At the top of each of the gold domes stands the star and crescent – a traditional symbol of Islam.

8 Ablutions
Two areas have faucets for worshipers to wash their hands, faces, and feet before prayers. Ablutions, or *wudhu* **(right)**, purify the body and soul.

10 ⭐ Sri Veeramakaliamman Temple

In the mid-19th century, Indian laborers who settled in what is now Little India built a Hindu shrine there. The original temple, a small nondescript structure, was demolished in 1983 to make way for the one that stands here today. It took three years to build, at great cost, with artisans brought from India. The temple is dedicated to the goddess Kali, who epitomizes the victory of good over evil. The name of the temple means 'Kali the Courageous'. This is one of Singapore's oldest holy sites.

1 Kali
Occupying the central position on the main altar, Kali **(above)** is the Divine Mother and Destroyer of Evil. She represents the cycle of birth through death – her name is Sanskrit for "endless time."

2 Muruga
This is the name given to the God of War – the six-headed deity who grants great success to his devotees. Muruga is worshipped mainly by Tamils, the majority of the city's Indians.

3 The Altar of the Nine Planets
Each single planet is represented on this altar at which devotees pray to their zodiac sign. Jewelry stores nearby sell rings adorned with nine stones, placed according to the astrological alignment of the wearer.

4 Ganesh
Distinguishable by his elephant's head, Ganesh **(right)** is the most worshipped of all Hindu deities. As the Remover of Obstacles, he is invoked at the start of prayers to help clear the mind, and consulted at the start of any new ventures.

5 Washing of the Deities
On the right side of the main altar, a small spout drains the water that rinsed the deities during their morning cleansing ritual. This holy water is used in prayer.

6 The Gopuram

Rows of figures, which are representations of deities, top the main gate (gopuram) and the roof **(below)**. On holy days, when the temple is full, devotees can appreciate them from outside.

7 Smashing Coconuts

Before entering the temple, devotees smash coconuts in a small metal box. This is symbolic of shattering their obstacles to spiritual concentration. These coconuts even have "eyes" carved into them, which are meant to "see" the obstacles in a devotee's path and destroy them.

ETIQUETTE IN HINDU TEMPLES

Visitors must remove footwear before they enter, and also wear appropriate attire – legs must be covered, and shirts should at least have short sleeves. In Indian culture, the left hand is reserved for toilet tasks, so pointing toward a person or sacred object with the left hand is impolite. If you must point, use your open hand. You should also turn off cell phones before entering.

9 Sri Lakshmi Durgai

While many Hindu figures and deities appear aggressive, Sri Lakshmi Durgai is represented as beautiful and graceful. According to Hindu belief, the goddess with three eyes and 18 arms will bring peace and joy to those devotees who pray to her.

8 Sri Periachi

In a corner, a dais holds the statue of the fierce Sri Periachi. Despite being depicted amid blood and gore, she is the goddess of fertility, childbirth, and the good health of newborns.

10 Roof Figures

On the main temple's roof are carved figures that tell stories from Hindu lore **(below)**, such as how Ganesh ended up with his elephant's head.

NEED TO KNOW

MAP F3 ▪ 141 Serangoon Rd ▪ 6295 4538 ▪ www.srivkt.org

Open 5:30am–9:30pm daily

▪ During Deepavali (see p67), the most significant holiday for local Hindus, the temple is illuminated with tiny candles, symbols of the eternal light of the soul.

▪ Suriya, a coffee shop nearby, at 140 Serangoon Rd, serves dosai (rice-flour pancakes) as well as good, cheap curries.

Following pages Detail of the gate to the Thian Hock Keng Temple

TOP10 ⭐ Singapore Botanic Gardens

This park is one of the finest botanical gardens in Southeast Asia and Singapore's sole UNESCO World Heritage Site. The park was founded in 1859 as a pleasure garden, and pathways meander through a tropical landscape that showcases the region's natural habitats and species. There are avenues of frangipanis and scarlet lipstick palms, and wide, sloping lawns adorned with trees and sculptures. On weekends, the park is packed with families, joggers, and dog walkers, but in the week, it is an oasis of calm.

1 National Orchid Garden

This beautiful enclosure *(see p47)* opened in 1995. It contains more than 1,000 orchid species **(right)** and 2,000 hybrids. Some hybrids are named in honor of visiting heads of state as well as international dignitaries. It is the only garden with an admission fee.

2 Vanda Miss Joaquim

There is debate over whether this hybrid of pink, violet, and orange-rose was discovered or bred by Miss Agnes Joaquim in 1893. It is a lovely orchid **(right)**, and was chosen as Singapore's national flower in 1981.

4 Healing Garden

This garden features more than 400 species of plants with healing properties. It is designed in the shape of a human body, and plants are then arranged thematically, in relation to where their efficacy lies.

3 The Lakes

The gardens have four lakes: Swan Lake **(left)**, with its white swans; Symphony Lake, where a stage hosts occasional concerts; Eco Lake; and the Keppel Discovery Wetlands, a tropical marsh environment.

5 Sculptures

Several sculptures in the gardens celebrate the families who come to play on weekends. Favorites include *Joy* **(left)**, overlooking Swan Lake, *The Girl on a Bicycle* who freewheels along the top of a spiral hedge, and *Girl on a Swing* who pauses mid-air.

6 Palm Valley

Developed in 1879, Palm Valley is home to more than 220 species of native and non-native palms arranged in "islands" representing the main palm sub-families. Among them are the large talipot palm and the traveler's palm, with its distinctive fan shape.

7 Children's Garden

At the Jacob Ballas Children's Garden, kids under the age of 12 years are encouraged to discover life sciences through play, and to investigate the role of plants and water in everyday life. Visitors should carry sunscreen and a change of clothing.

HENRY RIDLEY

Henry Ridley, a young British botanist, became the first director of the Botanic Gardens in 1888 and spent the next 23 years developing their horticultural potential. In the late 19th century, he devised a way to tap rubber without damaging the trees. Convinced of the crop's potential, he lobbied planters so zealously that he became known as "Mad Ridley."

9 Rain Forest

The park's first designers recognized the importance of the indigenous forest and preserved an area of rainforest, where ancient trees **(above)** continue to thrive today.

8 Bandstand

This octagonal structure was erected in the 1930s as a stage for performances by military bands. Although it no longer serves this purpose, it remains a central feature of the gardens.

10 The Ginger Garden

Several hundred kinds of ginger are displayed in this interesting garden, along with other ornamental and edible species **(left)**, including lilies and turmeric. The waterfall provides a great photo opportunity.

NEED TO KNOW

MAP S2 ■ 1 Cluny Rd ■ 6471-7361 ■ www.nparks.gov.sg/sbg

Open 5am–midnight daily

National Orchid Garden: open 8:30am–7pm daily; S$15 adults, S$3 senior citizens, free for under 12s

■ Free outdoor concerts take place at the Shaw Foundation Symphony Stage at weekends. Check the website or ask at the visitor service counters.

TOP 10 ⭐ Marina Bay

Built on reclaimed land, creating a freshwater reservoir in the process, the Marina Bay area offers great views of the cityscape. Besides being a part of Singapore's banking district, Marina Bay includes green spaces, notably Gardens by the Bay, as well as shopping malls and luxury residential high-rises. Most eye-catching is the giant boat-shaped structure on top of Marina Bay Sands resort, designed by Moshe Safdie, but surreal architectural marvels abound. Walking around the entirety of the Bay is possible along a 2-mile (3.5-km) waterfront promenade, crossing pedestrian bridges.

The impressive structure of Marina Bay Sands overlooking the cityscape

1 Gardens by the Bay

One of Singapore's top attractions, these extraordinary gardens (see pp28–9) contain over 1 million plants. The green towers of the Supertree Grove, two vast biodomes, free events, and excellent eating options keep visitors busy.

2 Esplanade – Theatres on the Bay

The spiked aluminum double-domes of the Esplanade host concerts, theater, dance, and visual arts events (see p42). The venue also has a library, an art gallery, shops, and restaurants. Makansutra (see p61) hawker center is also adjacent to it.

3 Marina Bay Sands

This integrated resort incorporates a five-star hotel (left), restaurants and nightlife, a casino, theaters, the ArtScience Museum, and The Shoppes luxury mall. On the 57th floor, there's an observation deck, an infinity pool, and a bar.

4 ArtScience Museum

Shaped like a lotus flower (above), this museum on the water's edge fuses design, science, and technology in its displays. Along with a permanent gallery, ten extended "fingers" host traveling science-themed exhibitions that are usually family-friendly.

5 Marina Barrage

This concrete dam can be crossed 24/7. The Sustainable Singapore Gallery – located on the western side of the dam – is free, with a huge grassy rooftop above that is popular with kite-flyers and picnickers.

6 The Skyline

Singapore's tallest skyscrapers, One Raffles Place, UOB Plaza One, and Republic Plaza, rise above Shenton Way, the city's downtown financial district, while the water's edge is flanked by low-rise heritage buildings.

7 Clifford Pier

Built in 1933, this Art Deco pier was the main landing point for sea travelers and, postwar, a departure point for ferries to minor offshore islands. Its soaring arches now form an airy restaurant serving top-notch local cuisine and afternoon tea.

8 Helix Bridge

Linking Marina South to Marina Centre, this curved-steel pedestrian bridge was inspired by the structure of DNA. It offers superb views of the Bay, particularly the ArtScience Museum, from its viewing platforms, and it is lit at night.

9 The Merlion

Half-fish and half-lion, the Merlion symbolizes the unity of the lion city and the sea. Guarding the Singapore River like an ancient mythical beast, the statue was unveiled in 1972.

SINGAPORE FLYER EXPERIENCES

For an unforgettable Flyer experience, there are three luxury options. The first two – the Singapore Sling Flight and the Premium Champagne Flight – are accompanied by a drink. The Sky Dining Flight offers a four-course Western, Chinese, or vegetarian meal, plus two rotations on the wheel.

10 Singapore Flyer

The largest observation wheel in Asia looms an impressive 541 ft (165 m) above Marina Bay. It offers expansive views over the Singapore River, from the Civic District out to the neighboring islands in the distance.

Marina Bay

NEED TO KNOW

Gardens by the Bay: MAP P4; 18 Marina Gardens Drive; 6420-6848; open 5–2am daily; Conservatories 9am–9pm daily; adm S$28 adults, S$15 children; www.gardensbythebay.com.sg

ArtScience Museum: MAP N3; 6 Bayfront Ave; 6688-8888; open10am–7pm daily; adm; www.marinabaysands.com

Sustainable Singapore Gallery: MAP T3; Marina Barrage, 8 Marina Gardens Drive; 6514-5959; open 9am–6pm Wed–Mon; www.pub.gov.sg/marinabarrage

Singapore Flyer: MAP P3; 30 Raffles Ave; 6333-3311; open 8:30am–10:30pm daily; adm S$33 adults, S$21

children (3–12 years old); www.singaporeflyer.com

■ The casino at Marina Bay Sands is free for foreigners. The dress code is smart casual – no beach wear, shorts, or flip flops.

■ The Sands Theatre at MBS offers great family entertainment, with musicals and touring Broadway shows.

TOP 10 ⭐ Gardens by the Bay

Stretching out over 250 acres (101 hectares) of green space on the Marina Bay waterfront, Gardens by the Bay features awe-inspiring conservatories, waterways, and aerial bridges. The Bay East and Bay Central gardens offer breathtaking views over the city's skyscrapers. Most of the attractions are in Bay South Garden, which also hosts festivals, music concerts, and community events. Home to more than a million plants, trees, and flowers from every continent but Antarctica, the Gardens are much loved by locals and visitors.

1 OCBC Skyway
Admire an incredible panorama of the Gardens toward Marina Bay from this 420-ft- (128-m-) long pathway, suspended 72 ft (22 m) above ground, between two Supertrees.

2 Heritage Gardens
These themed gardens reflect Singapore's varied cultures. The Indian Garden has been built in the shape of a traditional floral motif; the Malay Garden showcases various plants grown for food; and the Colonial Garden is fragrant with aromatic spices.

Picturesque view of the Gardens of the Bay

3 Cloud Forest
This conservatory **(below)** features a lush mountain and one of the world's tallest indoor waterfalls. Take a stroll on the aerial walkways and get up close to the plants.

4 Supertree Grove
With more than 200 plant species, these iconic vertical gardens collect and store rainwater, and harvest solar energy. The free Garden Rhapsody light-and-sound show *(see p64)* is held nightly here. Head to the Observatory at the top of the highest Supertree for captivating views of the city.

5 Sculptures
Over 40 indoor and outdoor sculptures are dotted throughout the garden. Keep an eye out for Dale Chihuly's *Ethereal White Persians* atop the Cloud Forest mountain, and Manolo Valdés's monumental bronze-and-iron *Ferns*.

8 Flower Dome

Nine gardens, including a Mediterranean garden, a South American garden, and a baobab grove, feature flora **(left)** from all over the globe in the world's largest glass greenhouse.

9 Floral Fantasy

Four themed landscapes – Dance, Float, Waltz, and Drift – form this graceful display of floral artworks, such as hanging bouquets, bubbling brooks, and dramatic driftwood sculptures. Visit Waltz, a vivarium, to see a colorful variety of tiny poison dart frogs.

10 Lakes

The two main lakes, Dragonfly and Kingfisher, are great for spotting dragonflies **(right)** among the reed beds. These lakes also create a natural filtration system for the Gardens' water runoff, which is cleansed by aquatic plants before it enters the Marina Reservoir.

SUSTAINABILITY

The vision behind these gardens are the principles of environmental sustainability. Carbon-neutral electricity is generated on site; energy-efficient technologies cool the conservatories; rare and endangered plants are a main highlight; and biodiverse ecosystems provide nursing environments and shelters for various fauna. In 2021, the Kingfisher Wetlands were built as a carbon sink: hundreds of mangrove plants, which capture and store more carbon than rainforests, help to mitigate the effects of global warming.

6 Kingfisher Wetlands

Streamlets, rock pools, and water cascades serve as microhabitats in this freshwater sanctuary. It includes more than 200 mangrove plants, some from endangered indigenous species. Spot birds and reptiles at the deck.

7 The Canyon

Find the world's largest collection of sculptural rocks here. Ancient rock forms sourced from Shandong, China, are placed along a 400-m (437-yard) trail.

NEED TO KNOW

MAP P3–5 ■ 18 Marina Gardens Drive ■ 6420-6040 ■ www.gardensbythebay.com.sg

Open 5–2am daily

OCBC Skyway: open 9am–9pm daily; adm S$8 adult, S$5 child, under 3s free

Cloud Forest and Flower Dome: open 9am–9pm daily; combo ticket adm S$28 adult, S$15 child, under-3s free

Supertree Observatory: open 4–9pm daily (from noon Sat, Sun & public hols); adm S$14 adult, S$10 child, under-3s free

Floral Fantasy: open 10am–7pm (until 8pm Sat, Sun & public hols); adm S$20 adult, S$12 child, under-3s free

■ A shuttle bus service runs at 10-minute intervals from Bayfront Plaza to the Flower Dome.

■ Try the seasonal dishes at Marguerite (www.marguerite.com.sg) set amid the lush garden of the Flower Dome.

■ Pack a picnic to enjoy on one of the wide lawns.

TOP 10 ⭐ Raffles Hotel

Behind the famous facade of Singapore's grandest hotel is a labyrinth of tropical courtyards and verandas. Raffles Hotel was founded by the Armenian Sarkies brothers in a beachfront bungalow in 1887. It was saved from demolition when it was declared a National Monument during its centennial – and multimillion-dollar renovations ensure the hotel maintains its late-1800s grandeur. With a range of restaurants, boutiques, galleries, bars, and a museum, Raffles is a destination in its own right.

1 Architectural Restoration

The Raffles Hotel known today was unveiled in 1991 after three years of restoration work costing S$160 million. Additional, extensive renovations from 2017 to 2019 have cemented the hotel's position as the grande dame of Singapore's luxury hotels.

2 The Raffles 1915 Gin

Commemorating the centenary of the popular Singapore Sling, this gin was created in association with London-based microdistillery Sipsmith, whose co-founder was a descendant of Sir Stamford Raffles.

3 Historical Charm

Character and opulence come at a price, but few hotels can match Raffles' blend of heritage and luxury. Beyond the entrance, guarded by liveried doormen in white turbans, are teak verandas, marble colonnades, and tropical gardens.

4 Writers Bar

The Writers Bar holds a series of books and other mementos of the hotel's literary heritage. There's also a gleaming brass counter, behind which staff prepare a range of delectable cocktails, some inspired by the hotel's first writer-in-residence, Pico Iyer.

Raffles Hotel exterior

5 Tiffin Room

In operation since 1892, the Tiffin Room is the hotel's highly esteemed North Indian curry house, serving spicy, aromatic buffet meals.

6 Raffles Boutique

The gift shop **(left)** sells teaspoons, safari hats, loose leaf tea, and other merchandise emblazoned with the Raffles palm motif or images of the facade. The boutique also has its own café, and hosts a heritage gallery showcasing the hotel's proud history.

8 The Long Bar

This must be the only bar **(left)** where guests are encouraged to litter peanut shells. It is the birthplace of the Singapore Sling, and still follows the original recipe but using premium ingredients.

CELEBRITY VISITORS

Raffles' celebrity guest list includes writers, singers, and actors from every era. The literary tradition began with Joseph Conrad and Rudyard Kipling, followed by Somerset Maugham. Guests from the entertainment world include Noël Coward, Ava Gardner as well as Michael Jackson and Elizabeth Taylor, who arrived together in 1993. Cate Blanchett and Glenn Close visited in 1996 while filming the movie *Paradise Road* here.

10 Raffles Courtyard

Guests sip cocktails surrounded by lush plants and ornate fixtures in this open-air bar – one of the most popular areas of the hotel.

7 Osteria BBR by Alain Ducasse

One of several restaurants helmed by big-name chefs, Osteria BBR **(below)** is housed in the historic bar and billiards room. It offers an upscale Italian menu and a hearty Sunday brunch, accompanied by prosecco.

9 Afternoon Tea at the Grand Lobby

The most refined of all traditions at Raffles Hotel is the afternoon tea **(right)**. Finger sandwiches, scones with clotted cream, and pastries accompany a special coffee blend or a range of specialty teas.

NEED TO KNOW

MAP M1 ■ 1 Beach Rd ■ 6337-1886 ■ www. raffles.com/singapore

Tiffin Room: open daily

Raffles Boutique: 6412-1143; open 10am–7:30pm daily

Osteria BBR by Alain Ducasse: open noon– 2:30pm & 6–9:15pm Thu–Mon

Raffles Courtyard: open 3–10pm daily

■ Some venues have a smart-casual dress code.

TOP 10 ★ Sentosa

Sentosa is Singapore's pleasure island – a local getaway dedicated to recreation. The landscape is still being added to and there is something for everyone here – the most well-known draw is Universal Studios. Pleasant artificial beaches lie alongside lush wooded slopes, with plenty of bars and restaurants nearby. The island was originally called Pulau Blakang Mati, meaning "death from behind," possibly because of the pirates that once attacked its shores. It was later renamed Sentosa, which means "peace and tranquility."

1 S.E.A. Aquarium

Housing stunningly vast tanks **(below)**, this slick aquarium focuses on the diverse life in the waters surrounding Asia. The showstopper is the Open Ocean zone, home to sharks and manta rays.

2 Images of Singapore

This exhibit, along with the accompanying Spirit of Singapore boat ride, traces the nation's history – from a humble fishing village to a 21st-century powerhouse.

3 Skypark Sentosa

Towering over Siloso Beach, adventure sports company A. J. Hackett's 50-meter tower was purpose-built for bungy jumping. It also includes a giant swing as well as a Skybridge with transparent sections.

NEED TO KNOW

MAP S3 ■ Sentosa Island ■ 1800-736-8672 ■ www.sentosa.com.sg

Open 24 hours daily

■ To reach Sentosa, take the Sentosa Express monorail from VivoCity mall, or catch Bus 123 from Orchard Road. If you take a taxi, there is a small charge in addition to the metered fare.

■ Transport at Sentosa, including shuttle buses, is free except for cable-car rides.

■ Coastes (www.coastes. com) serves drinks and food all day long.

Sentosa

6 Siloso Beach

This beach (left) is where the jetset hang out, sunbathing and playing volleyball. Several bars and restaurants operate during the day, although the pace (and volume) picks up at sunset.

7 Sofitel Spa

Set in a tropical garden featuring waterfalls and volcanic mud pools, Sofitel spa has 14 indoor treatment rooms, six outdoor pavilions, and a variety of facilities for guests to choose from.

4 Sentosa 4D AdventureLand

Billed as a theme park, this is Southeast Asia's first 4D theater. AdventureLand features a state-of-the-art digital projection system, surround-sound, and seats that move with the on-screen action. The effects include mist spray in water scenes.

5 Fort Siloso

Original features here (see p44) recreate the life of WWII soldiers. Special effects include battle sounds and recreations of Japan's surrender.

8 Skyline Luge Sentosa

A cross between a toboggan and a go-cart, the luge (left) is great fun for all ages. Take the Skyride chair-lift to the top of the hill and whiz back down again as fast as you dare. Each cart has sophisticated speed controls for safety and children can ride tandem with an adult.

9 Singapore Cable Car

The glass cabins of the cable car offer a pricey but exciting way to arrive at Sentosa from Mount Faber (see p100) via Harbour Front. From its Imbiah Lookout terminus, a branch line (below) takes you to the western tip of the island.

10 Mega Adventure Park

There's a choice of four challenges here, including a rope-based obstacle course, but the most captivating of all is the 1,476-ft- (450-m-) long zip line which will have you soaring over Siloso Beach.

The Top 10
of Everything

Bridges spanning the atrium of
the National Gallery Singapore

🔟 Moments in History

1 1390: Iskandar Shah

Singapore was first inhabited by the Indigenous Orang Laut people, and by the 1200s, it was known as Temasek. Legend has it that in 1390, a Sumatran prince called Iskandar Shah declared himself ruler of Temasek. After spotting a lion-like creature, he renamed the island Singapura, or lion island. The Keramat at Fort Canning is said to be his tomb *(see p47)*.

2 1400s–1500s: Trading Post

At the end of the 14th century, Singapura came under attack from the Javanese or Siamese. Singapura was ruled by the Sultanate of Malacca and then by the Sultanate of Johor. It soon became a small trading post.

3 1819: Arrival of Sir Stamford Raffles

After arriving at Singapore, Lieutenant-Governor Stamford Raffles established a trading port on behalf of the English East India Company in 1819.

4 1824: British East India Company

The East India Company secured legal rule of the island following an Anglo-Dutch treaty. In 1826, Singapore was declared capital of the Straits Settlements and became a flourishing Crown Colony by 1867.

Japanese aircrafts attack Singapore

Worker tapping a rubber tree

5 1907: Rubber and Tin

New technologies demanded new materials. Rubber seedlings grown in the Botanic Gardens *(see pp24–5)* gave rise to Singapore's first rubber plantation. The first smelter for producing tin opened at Pulau Brani to satisfy the demands of America's new canning industry.

6 1942–5: Japanese Occupation

During World War II Singapore was attacked by Japanese aircrafts. It fell to the Japanese on February 15, 1942, and an estimated 50,000 people, mainly Chinese Singaporeans, died during the three-year Japanese occupation of the island. When the Japanese surrendered in 1945, the island was handed over to the British Military Administration.

7 1959: Singapore's Self-Government

After many years of negotiation, the British agreed to hold general elections, resulting in a landslide victory for the People's Action Party, which promised a Singapore united with Malaya and fully independent of Britain.

8 1959: Lee Kuan Yew

Lee Kuan Yew became the island's first prime minister on June 3, 1959. Revered by Singaporeans as the father of the nation, Lee remained a towering figure in Asian politics until his death in 2015.

First prime minister, Lee Kuan Yew

9 1965: Singapore's Independence

Singapore became part of the Federation of Malaysia in 1963. However, political and racial tensions led to riots in 1964, and, on August 9, 1965, Lee announced a separation from Malaysia and the Republic of Singapore was born.

10 2017: Halimah Yacob becomes President

Halimah Yacob is the first female president of Singapore and the only Malay to be elected for the role in 47 years.

TOP 10 SINGAPORE READS

The graphic novelist Sonny Liew

1 *Singapore: A Biography* **by Mark Ravinder Frost and Yu-Mei Balasingamchow**
Singapore's history recounted by its revolutionaries, laborers, and rulers.

2 *Inheritance* **by Balli Kaur Jaswal**
A rich portrait of tradition, identity, and belonging in an evolving Singapore.

3 *Abraham's Promise* **by Philip Jeyaretnam**
An elderly teacher reminisces about his youth in 1950s and 1960s Singapore.

4 *The Art of Charlie Chan Hock Chye* **by Sonny Liew**
A multi-layered graphic novel recounts 80 years of Singapore's history.

5 *Or Else, The Lightning God and Other Stories* **by Catherine Lim**
Keenly observed vignettes of life in Singapore during the 1970s.

6 *Crazy Rich Asians* **by Kevin Kwan**
A satire about the schemes of three wealthy Chinese families in Singapore.

7 *Singapore Noir* **edited by Cheryl Lu-Lien Tan**
Portrays Singapore's gritty back alleys, gambling dens, and red-light districts.

8 *Balik Kampung* **edited by Verena Tay**
Explores Singapore's neighborhoods in a collection of short stories.

9 *Saving the Rainforest and Other Stories* **by Claire Tham**
Riveting scenes of everyday life in Singapore.

10 *State of Emergency* **by Jeremy Tiang**
Family history and the history of a nation are woven together in this novel.

🔟 Places of Worship

1 St. Andrew's Cathedral

Named for the patron saint of Scotland, this Anglican church (see p43) is on a piece of land selected by Raffles himself. Inside the church is the Canterbury Stone, presented by the Metropolitan Cathedral Church of Canterbury. The Coventry Cross is made of silver-plated nails from the ruins of Coventry Cathedral, and the Coronation Carpet is part of the one used for Queen Elizabeth II in Westminster Abbey.

2 Armenian Church

MAP L2 ■ 60 Hill St ■ 6334-0141 ■ Open 10am–6pm daily ■ www.armeniansinasia.org

Built in 1835 and devoted to St. Gregory the Illuminator, this church was the focal point for an Armenian community. Gravestones installed in the grounds commemorate prominent community members such as the Sarkies brothers who founded the Raffles Hotel and the lady for whom the national flower, the Vanda Miss Joaquim, is named.

3 CHIJMES (Convent of the Holy Infant Jesus)

This former convent school (see p43) is now an entertainment complex. It contains an ornate Gothic chapel

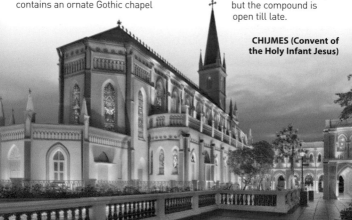

that still hosts weddings and was also featured in the film *Crazy Rich Asians*. A door in the north-east corner of the grounds is the spot where abandoned babies were left to be cared for by the nuns.

Sri Thendayuthapani Temple statue

4 Sri Thendayutha-pani Temple

MAP K1 ■ 15 Tank Rd ■ 6737-9393 ■ Open 8am–noon & 5:30–8:30pm daily ■ www.sttemple.com

This Hindu temple had humble beginnings as a statue of Lord Muruga under a bodhi tree. A permanent temple was built in 1859 but it was replaced by a new one in 1983. It is renovated every 12 years, in keeping with Hindu tradition.

5 Kong Meng San Phor Kark See Temple

MAP T2 ■ 88 Bright Hill Rd ■ 6849-5300 ■ Open 8am–4pm daily ■ www.kmspks.org

The largest Buddhist temple in Singapore, this 1920 complex was built to house the growing numbers of monks residing in the city. It continues to be an important monastery. The Hall of Great Strength closes at 4pm and the Hall of Great Compassion at 4:45pm, but the compound is open till late.

CHIJMES (Convent of the Holy Infant Jesus)

6 Cathedral of the Good Shepherd

MAP M1 ■ A Queen St ■ 6337-2036 ■ Open 8am–9pm Mon–Fri (from 7am Sat & Sun) ■ www.cathedral.catholic.sg

Catholicism arrived with the Portuguese in the 1500s. Singapore's early days saw Catholic services being held in a thatched structure at Bras Basah Road. By the mid-1800s, this church had been built, along with two schools, St. Joseph's Institution and the Convent of the Holy Infant Jesus, all within close proximity. The cathedral has been impeccably restored, and non-Catholics are welcome for mass.

Altar at Tan Si Chong Su Temple

7 Maghain Aboth Synagogue

MAP L1 ■ 24 Waterloo St ■ 6337-2189 ■ Adm by prior arrangement ■ www.singaporejews.com

Jews first arrived in Singapore from Iran and Iraq in 1831. Their oldest synagogue in Singapore, Maghain Aboth or "shield of our fathers," was consecrated in 1878.

8 Telok Ayer Chinese Methodist Church

MAP L5 ■ 235 Telok Ayer St ■ 6324-4001 ■ Open 9am–5pm daily ■ www.tacmc.org.sg

Hokkien Methodists built the church in 1924. Many details, such as the windows and arches, are of their time, while the roof line is distinctly traditional Chinese. Services are held in Chinese, Hokkien, and Mandarin dialects.

9 Tan Si Chong Su Temple

MAP K3 ■ 15 Magazine Rd ■ 6533-2880 ■ Open 9am–11pm daily

This shrine is dedicated to the Tan family clan. It was originally built on the riverside, but due to land reclamation, it now lies well away from the water's edge.

Behind the temple, a private hall encloses ancestral tablets of deceased clan members.

10 Hong San See Temple

MAP J2 ■ 31 Mohammed Sultan Rd ■ 6737-3683

Built on a hill above Mohammed Sultan Road, this 100-year-old temple complex was erected by migrants from the Fujian province in China. Inside the entrance hall are granite plaques listing the donors who contributed to the building. The temple is dedicated to the God of Fortune, the Goddess of Mercy, and the Heavenly Emperor. It was designated as a national monument in Singapore in 1978.

🔟 Museums

1 National Gallery Singapore

MAP M2 ■ 1 St. Andrew's Rd ■ 6271-7000 ■ Open 10am–7pm daily ■ Adm ■ www.nationalgallery.sg

Opened in 2015, this gallery houses a fine permanent and traveling collection of local and East Asian artwork.

National Gallery Singapore

2 Peranakan Museum

MAP L1 ■ 39 Armenian St ■ 6332-7591 ■ Closed for renovation until 2023 ■ Adm ■ www.peranakanmuseum.org.sg

This museum explores the culture of the Peranakans, people born of intermarriage between local women and foreign traders from countries such as China and India. The mix of two distinct communities is seen in a range of spectacular works of art – jewelry, furniture, beadwork, porcelain, and other treasures.

3 Lee Kong Chian Natural History Museum

2 Conservatory Drive, National University of Singapore ■ 6601-3333 ■ Open 10am–6pm Tue–Sun ■ Adm: adults S\$21, students and senior citizens S\$13 ■ www.lkcnhm.nus.edu.sg

One of Singapore's best-kept secrets, this museum houses a splendid collection of biological specimens illustrating the marvelous diversity of nature. There's also useful background on Singapore's flora, fauna, and geology.

4 Malay Heritage Centre

MAP H4 ■ 85 Sultan Gate ■ 6391-0450 ■ Open 10am–6pm Tue–Sun (last adm 5:30pm) ■ Adm ■ www.malayheritage.org.sg

Formely a palace used by royals of the Johor sultanate, the Malay Heritage Centre was redeveloped in 2005. It features permanent galleries, covering the history of the neighborhood, Kampong Glam. It also elucidates the culture and contributions of the Malay community.

5 Changi Chapel and Museum

MAP U2 ■ 1000 Upper Changi Rd ■ 6242-6033 ■ Open 9:30am–5:30pm Tue–Sun ■ Adm ■ www.nhb.gov.sg/changichapelmuseum

This museum reopened in 2021 after major renovation. It commemorates the World War II prisoner-of-war camp for Allied troops and civilians that was housed at Changi Prison.

6 Chinatown Heritage Centre

MAP K4 ■ 48 Pagoda St ■ 6224-3928 ■ Open 9:30am–6pm daily ■ Adm ■ www.chinatown.sg

Dioramas re-create the conditions in which early Chinese immigrants lived. Families were packed into cubicles, and battled poverty, disease, and opium addiction.

Chinatown Heritage Centre

Exhibits in the National Museum of Singapore

7 National Museum of Singapore

Dating back to 1849, Singapore's oldest museum (see pp12–13) tells the island's whirlwind story from the 14th century to the present. The various exhibits are interesting to visitors of all ages, and history buffs can enjoy additional information on the museum app.

8 Asian Civilisations Museum

Asian Civilisations Museum artifact

Housed in the former Empress Place Building, this museum (see pp14–15) explores the history, art, and culture of Asia, with 1,300 artifacts that include Indonesian shrines, Islamic art, and textiles.

9 Red Dot Design Museum

MAP N5 ■ 11 Marina Boulevard ■ www.museum.red-dot.sg

Asia's largest design museum has over 1,000 contemporary design and communication products. Among the innovative items on show are winners of the Red Dot Design Award, one of the world's most renowned design competitions.

10 Former Ford Factory

MAP S2 ■ 351 Upper Bukit Timah Rd ■ Open 9am–5:30pm Tue–Sun ■ Adm ■ www.nas.gov.sg/formerfordfactory

Occupying the former car factory where, in 1942, British forces surrendered to the Japanese, this war museum is run by Singapore's National Archives. It exhibits a wide variety of documents and artifacts that evoke the harshness of life under occupation, as well as to explore the post-war clamour for independence.

TOP 10 Architectural Sights

The durian-like structure of the Esplanade with the Singapore Flyer behind

1 Old Parliament House

Singapore's oldest building, dating from 1827, was mistakenly built as a private residence on a spot reserved for government use and subsequently taken over by the colonial administration (see p15). Designed by G. D. Coleman, the Neo-Palladian-style building incorporates verandas and high ceilings. In 2003, it was converted to The Arts House, a venue for exhibitions, recitals, and other events.

2 The Esplanade – Theatres on the Bay

MAP N2–N3 ■ 1 Esplanade Drive ■ 6828-8377 ■ Open 10am–11pm daily ■ www.esplanade.com

Built at a cost of S$600 million, the Esplanade opened in 2002 amid debate over its aesthetic worth. The aluminum shades encasing its domes inspire locals to call it "the Durian."

3 Emerald Hill Road

Pre-war row houses lining this road (see p95) were some of the earliest to be conserved as private residences. Their architecture illustrates the cultural influences of the 1900s. Houses of note are at numbers 41, 77, and 79–81.

4 City Hall and Supreme Court

MAP M2 ■ 3 St. Andrew's Rd

Both buildings impress from the outside – City Hall with its columns and wide steps, and the old Supreme Court with its dome. The two now form the National Gallery (see p40). Visitors can view the chamber where the Japanese signed their surrender in 1945, as well as the court's marbled corridors and courtrooms.

5 St. Andrew's Cathedral
MAP M2 ■ 11 St. Andrew's Rd ■ 6337-6104 ■ Open 9am–5pm Mon–Sat ■ www.cathedral.org.sg

Resembling an English parish church, this Anglican church, consecrated in 1862, is made of *chunam*, a paste of shell lime, egg whites, and coarse sugar mixed with boiled coconut husks. The recipe was imported from British India and applied by Indian convict laborers.

6 Empress Place Building
In 1867, the government built the Empress Place to house its administrative offices. Placed at the mouth of the Singapore River (see pp14–15), the Neo-Palladian structure was one of the first things newcomers to the city would see on arrival. In the 1980s, it was initially converted into an art museum, and after several major extensions in the 1990s, it became home to a wing of the Asian Civilisations Museum.

7 The Istana and Sri Temasek
The Istana, which means "palace" in Malay, was built in 1869 as a governor's residence (see p94). Situated on a hilltop, it is a blend of traditional Malay palace design and Italian Renaissance decor. Sri Temasek, a smaller building in the compound, was built for colonial officers.

The colorful exterior of Tan House

8 House of Tan Teng Niah
MAP F4 ■ 37 Kerbau Rd ■ No public access

Known as Tan House, this house was built in 1900 and is a mix of cultural influences, with European columns and arched windows, Chinese green tiles, and Malay wooden detailing. It now houses offices.

9 Victoria Theatre and Concert Hall
This ornate structure was built in the Italian Renaissance style popular in Victorian England at the time (see p89). The theater was finished in 1862. In 1905, the Memorial Hall was added to honor Queen Victoria.

10 CHIJMES (Convent of the Holy Infant Jesus)
MAP M1 ■ 30 Victoria St ■ Open 8am–midnight daily (clubs open till late) ■ www.chijmes.com.sg

This convent was originally built in 1841, and an orphanage was added in 1856. In 1903, a chapel was added, lending a Gothic touch with arches and columns. In the 1990s, the convent made way for clubs and restaurants.

Empress Place Building extension

🔟 World War II Sights

The Surrender Chamber at Fort Siloso

1 Fort Siloso

The last British coastal fort on Sentosa *(see pp32–3)* offers an insight into the lives of World War II soldiers. The Surrender Chamber recreates the 1945 British and Japanese surrenders.

2 Reflections at Bukit Chandu

MAP S3 ▪ 31-K Pepys Rd ▪ 6375-2510 ▪ Open 9:30am–5pm Tue–Sun ▪ Adm ▪ www.nhb.gov.sg/bukitchandu

In February 1942, 1,400 soldiers of the Malay Regiment took a stand on Bukit Chandu against 13,000 Japanese soldiers. This museum recounts the battle and the courage displayed by the soldiers.

3 Labrador Park

MAP S3 ▪ Labrador Villa Rd ▪ Open 7am–7pm daily

Guns capable of firing shells almost 10 miles (16 km) were installed at Fort Pasir Panjang to help protect it from attack by sea. Many of the gun emplacements can still be seen.

Kranji War Memorial and Cemetery

4 Battlebox

MAP E6 ▪ 2 Cox Terrace ▪ 6338-6133 ▪ Open for pre-booked tours only (9:30am–5:30pm Fri–Sun & public hols) ▪ www.battlebox.com.sg

The museum is housed in what was the British World War II command center, which was designed to be bombproof and capable of recycling its air supply. Models depict the 1942 meeting, during which General Percival decided to surrender to the Japanese.

5 Changi Chapel and Museum

This museum *(see p40)* is dedicated to those held at Changi Prison and camp from 1942 to 1945, and features replicas of the murals painted in St. Luke's Chapel by Bombardier Stanley Warren.

6 Former Ford Factory

The former Ford factory *(see p41)* features an exhibition organized by the National Archives of Singapore. The displays present a detailed look into the lives of the locals before, during, and after World War II, as well as tell the story of the Singapore's Japanese occupation and subsequent struggle for independence.

7 Kranji War Memorial and Cemetery

This memorial *(see p103)* stands over the graves of more than 4,000 Allied servicemen lost in battle here. The pillars list the names of 24,000 others whose bodies were not found.

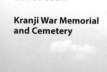

8 The Padang

This is the downtown "playing field" where Japanese troops gathered and divided the European population. British and Australian soldiers were to be held at the Selarang Barracks, while 2,300 civilians were sent to Changi Prison. After the Japanese surrendered to the British, a victory parade was held here.

MAJOR WORLD WAR II EVENTS IN SINGAPORE

General Percival surrenders

1 December 7–8, 1941
The Japanese attacked Pearl Harbor and then launched a huge offensive, invading the Philippines, Hong Kong, and Thailand, and dropping the first bombs on Singapore.

2 February 8, 1942
Japan invaded Singapore from the north by crossing the causeway.

3 February 15, 1942
British General Percival surrendered to General Yamashito of Japan, and the Japanese occupation began.

4 February 16, 1942
The European population assembled at the Padang, before being marched 14 miles (23 km) to Changi Prison.

5 May 1943
The first group of 600 prisoners was dispatched to work on the notorious Burma-Thailand "death railway."

6 1943
Wartime rations were cut as the war turned against Japan and living conditions began to worsen.

7 November 1944
Starvation and disease were widespread. The US carried out its first raid on the Singapore harbor.

8 Early 1945
Living conditions became almost unbearable, with many people dying of malnutrition and disease.

9 May 1945
News of the end of the European War reached Singapore – the end was near for the desperate city.

10 September 12, 1945
Japan surrendered to Lord Mountbatten, the last British Viceroy of India, in a formal ceremony at Singapore's City Hall.

Pillars at the Civilian War Memorial

9 Civilian War Memorial

MAP M2 ■ War Memorial Park, Beach Rd

Locally known as the "chopsticks," the four pillars here symbolize the races (Chinese, Malay, Indian, and others) that suffered during the Japanese occupation. Remains of unidentified victims are buried at the base of the monument.

10 Lim Bo Seng Memorial

MAP M3 ■ Esplanade Park

This monument is a tribute to Chinese resistance fighter Lim Bo Seng, who escaped to Sri Lanka right before the Japanese invasion. He returned to the Malay Peninsula, in secret, to help organize the resistance movement but was captured and died in captivity.

🔟 National Parks and Gardens

1 Singapore Botanic Gardens

Although Orchard Road is just a short walk away, the city seems deceptively distant when you are surrounded by frangipani (plumeria) trees, lakes, and rainforest. A walk through the tranquil gardens (see pp24–5) is the perfect follow-up to a day of sightseeing or shopping. Locals may be seen practicing Tai Chi on the lawns in the morning.

2 Chinese and Japanese Gardens

Reopened in 2022 after a major revamp are a pair of gardens (see p101) on adjoining islands on Jurong Lake, in the western region of Singapore. The Chinese Garden features an excellent Suzhou-style bonsai collection, colorful buildings, and a stone boat. Steps away, over the Bridge of Double Beauty, the Japanese Garden is the essence of serenity. Enjoy the view of both from the top of the Chinese Garden's seven-story pagoda.

3 The Southern Ridges

These forested ridges (see p100) along Singapore's southwest coast comprise four interconnected parks stretching more than 6 miles (10 km), linked by pathways and bridges.

Sungei Buloh Wetland Reserve

4 Sungei Buloh Wetland Reserve

Boardwalk trails wind through this reserve (see p101) among mangroves that are home to mudskippers and monitor lizards. Look out for salt-water crocodiles and the Atlas moth, one of the largest in the world, with a wingspan of up to 1 ft (0.3 m). Hides by the pools allow you to observe some of the 144 bird species found here.

5 Gardens by the Bay

Spanning a huge area, Gardens by the Bay (see pp28–9) is an award-winning Singapore park, comprising three waterfront gardens – Bay South Garden, Bay East Garden, and Bay Central Garden. The main attraction, Bay South Garden, has popular features such as the Flower Dome, the Cloud Forest, and the Supertree Grove. The park also hosts various events

The sprawling Gardens by the Bay

and is a popular destination among people of all ages.

6 East Coast Park

MAP T3 ■ East Coast Parkway ■ www.nparks. gov.sg

For many visitors, this park is their first glimpse of Singapore, stretching along the expressway from the airport to the city. The long strip of sandy beach with paths shaded by casuarina trees and coconut palms is popular with bicyclists and rollerbladers. From here, the countless ships plying the Strait make for an incongruous sight.

7 MacRitchie Nature Trail

MAP S2 ■ Off Lornie Rd ■ Open daily ■ www. nparks.gov.sg

Vestiges of the city-state's rubber plantations can be witnessed from the boardwalk encircling this reservoir park. Trails through the forest range in length from 2 to 7 miles (3 to 11 km). The 82-ft- (25-m-) high treetop walk offers many spectacular views of the lush forest canopy.

National Orchid Garden

8 National Orchid Garden

The Botanic Gardens house a collection of more than 1,000 orchid species and 2,000 hybrids (see pp24–5). It has different environments for each group of orchids and bromeliads. The Coolhouse offers a welcome respite from the year-round heat of the city.

9 Fort Canning Park

Called "Forbidden Hill" originally, this park is said to be the site of the tomb of Iskandar Shah, who first settled in Singapore. Raffles built his bungalow here but, in 1859, it was replaced by a military base and renamed Fort Canning. The fort became the British headquarters in the Battle for Singapore. Raffles designated it the island's first botanic garden (see p90). In 2019, new gardens were launched to commemorate Singapore's bicentennial.

10 Mount Imbiah Nature Trail

Given its short distance and well-graded paths, this walking trail in Sentosa (see pp32–3) is one of the easiest ways for children or beginners to glimpse Singapore's forest. However, it is not accessible for strollers and wheelchairs.

🔟 Spas

1 Willow Stream Spa

MAP M1 ■ Fairmont Singapore, 80 Bras Basah Rd ■ 6431-5600 ■ Open 7am–9pm daily ■ www.fairmont.com/singapore/spa/willow-stream-spa-singapore/

This spa is a haven of soft music and earth tones. For a full-body pampering experience, book in for one of the Willow Streams Experiences, such as the Jetsetter Recovery Massage, which begins with a eucalyptus foot bath before an energizing massage with a blend of essential oils.

Swimming pool at Sofitel Spa

2 Sofitel Spa

MAP S3 ■ Sofitel Singapore Sentosa, 2 Bukit Manis Rd ■ 6708-8358 ■ Open 10am–9pm daily (last adm 8pm) ■ www.sofitel-singapore-sentosa.com

Located in the heart of Sentosa Island, this spa is built on a vast 64,580 sq ft (6,000 sq m) heritage site. It has six outdoor pavilions besides 14 indoor treatment rooms. A choice of options allows guests to customize sessions.

3 The Face Place

MAP L3 ■ #12–83 Clarke Quay Central, 8 Eu Tong Sen St ■ 8233-1723 ■ Open 9am–9pm daily ■ www.thefaceplacesg.com

Overlooking the Singapore River, this spa specializes in facial massages and treatments. The signature spa uses *Gua Sha* and *Bojin* techniques that stimulate facial muscles. It offers bespoke treatments as well, such as double cleansing and skin analysis.

4 Banyan Tree Spa

MAP N4 ■ Level 55, Tower 1, Marina Bay Sands, 10 Bayfront Ave ■ 6688-8825 ■ Open 10am–11pm Sun–Thu (until 1am Fri & Sat) ■ www.banyantreespa.com

One of the loftiest spas on the island, Banyan Tree has stunning views over the city center. There are traditional Asian massages as well as customized ones, and treatments such as the Royal Banyan, featuring cucumber cleanser, and a blissful herbal bath.

5 Damai Spa

MAP B3 ■ Grand Hyatt Singapore, 10 Scotts Rd ■ 6416-7156 ■ Closed for renovation until 2023 ■ www.hyatt.com

Part of the hotel's new Wellness Wing, complete with a five-story cascading garden and waterfall feature, the revamped Damai Spa offers a variety of signature treatments, as well as essential services.

6 Spa Esprit

MAP S3 ■ #03–19 Wheelock Place, 501 Orchard Rd ■ 6479-0070 ■ Open 10am–9pm daily ■ www.spa-esprit.com

After a long, cramped flight, head to this branch of Spa Esprit

Nail products at Spa Esprit at HOUSE

A couple enjoying a massage at The Spa at Mandarin Oriental, Singapore

for a hot stone massage. A therapist will soften your muscle tissue with heated stones and ease tight spots with a series of deep, intensive strokes. Emerge relaxed and ready for a drink at the in-house bar.

7 Ikeda Spa
787 Bukit Timah Rd ■ 6469-8080 ■ Open 1:30–10:30pm daily ■ www.ikedaspa.com

The spa recreates the traditional Japanese ryokan bath-house experience in luxurious style. There's a communal bath with mineral-enriched water and a wide range of massages, as well as treatments.

8 Auriga
MAP S3 ■ Capella Singapore, 1 The Knolls, Sentosa Island ■ 6377 8888 ■ Open 9am–9pm daily ■ www.capella hotels.com/en/capella-singapore/wellness

Set amid lush greenery, this luxury spa is the perfect oasis for a vacation. It features a vitality pool, herbal steam room, and nine treatment rooms with private gardens. There are regionally inspired treatments as well, including Balinese and Ayurvedic massages.

9 The Spa at Mandarin Oriental, Singapore
MAP N2 ■ Mandarin Oriental, Singapore, 5 Raffles Ave ■ 6885-3533 ■ Open 9:30am–7pm Thu–Mon ■ www.mandarinoriental.com/singa pore/marina-bay/luxury-spa

This intimate haven of healing, relaxation, and calm has six treatment rooms and offers a range of results-driven therapies.

10 St. Gregory Spa
MAP K3 ■ PARKROYAL Collection Pickering, 3 Upper Pickering St ■ 6809-8870 ■ Open 10:30am–8pm daily

Part of PARKROYAL's dedicated wellness floor, this spa offers a wide range of treatments as well as massages, including the Chinese tui na.

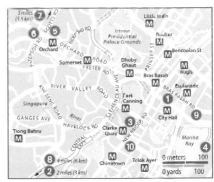

🔟 Off the Beaten Path

as sea kayaking and dragon-boat racing. The state-of-the-art Singapore Sports Hub, on the east bank, comprises the National Stadium and Sports Museum, and has excellent dining for all price budgets. Kallang Riverside Park is a lovely stroll from the Singapore Flyer, along the palm-lined Marina Promenade.

① Black-and-White Houses

Dotted around Singapore are little pockets of colonial-era black-and-white houses, with sweeping grounds dating from the late 19th century to the 1930s. Wessex Estate in Queenstown is ideal to explore, with Art Deco bungalows and flats, and an artist community. Finish with refreshments in time-warp ColBar, a no-frills joint that used to be a military canteen. Nearby Alexandra Park has more grand black-and-white mansions.

② Kallang River Basin

www.sportshub.com.sg

Kallang River flows into this basin, creating a hub for sports such

③ Bollywood Farms

MAP R1 ▪ **100 Neo Tiew Rd** ▪ **www.bollywood veggies.com.sg**

Connect with the land at this organic farm in Kranji countryside. Owners Ivy Lim-Singh and Lim Ho Seng organize farm tours and various activities. The on-site bistro serves local dishes showcasing the farm's harvest, and visitors can buy chemical-free produce such as *kedongdong* (a tropical fruit) in the farm shop.

④ St. John's, Lazarus, and Kusu Islands

Singapore Island Cruise: www. islandcruise.com.sg

Take a picnic to visit these tiny islands off Singapore's south coast. There are white-sand beaches, walking trails, a vibrant Chinese temple, a tortoise sanctuary, and sacred Malay shrines – and on a

Pier on Kusu Island

weekday, they are all blissfully quiet. There are usually at least four ferry departures a day to Kusu Island via St. John's Island, which is connected to Lazarus by a causeway.

5 Changi Point Coastal Walk
MAP V1 ■ Open 24 hours

Stroll east from Changi Point along this boardwalk tracing the coastline, and Singapore will suddenly feel like a sleepy little island. It gives views across the sea to Pulau Ubin and Malaysia, culminating at a sunset spot. There are great food options at Changi Village, near the Point.

6 Everton Road
MAP J5

This charming road and its adjacent streets are pristine examples of colorful Peranakan row houses. Murals by local resident Mr. Yip Yew Chong decorate some of the walls, depicting the Singaporean life of yesteryear. The local coffee shops are highly rated.

A craft market organized by Invade

7 Craft Markets
Invade: www.invade.co

Singapore may be famous for high-end fashion stores and luxury shopping malls, but the city also has a plethora of immensely popular markets that offer a wide range of crafts, local produce, vintage fashion, and many more products. Invade regularly organizes makers' markets, thrift markets, and flea markets across several locations around the city.

National University of Singapore

8 National University of Singapore and Lee Kong Chian Natural History Museum

The free NUS Museum (see p54) has a collection of more than 8,000 Southeast Asian artifacts, and changing art and archaeology exhibitions. Also on site is the excellent Lee Kong Chian Natural History Museum (see p40) (admission charge), with 20 zones of regional animal specimens and dinosaurs. Although partly interactive, the museum harks back to the days of wooden display cases including cabinets of curiosities.

9 Coney Island Park
MAP U1 ■ www.nparks.gov.sg

Off Singapore's northern coast, this unspoiled casuarina-covered island is connected to the mainland by two bridges. It has walking trails, bike tracks, tiny beaches, and a mangrove boardwalk.

10 Punggol Waterway Park
MAP T1 ■ www.nparks.gov.sg

The new town of Punggol is dense with shiny high-rises, but interwoven with a landscaped waterway park and promenade. Impressive bridges, nature, recreation areas, and heritage zones help create a sense of a waterfront town.

🔟 Children's Attractions

Visitors riding the flumes at Wild Wild Wet

① Wild Wild Wet

MAP U2 ▪ 1 Pasir Ris Close
▪ 6581-9128 ▪ Open noon–6pm
Wed–Mon (from 10am Sat, Sun &
public holidays) ▪ Adm ▪ www.wild
wildwet.com

Get soaked on the flumes, water
mazes, and the Royal Flush –
Asia's first hybrid water ride.

② Universal Studios Singapore®

MAP S3 ▪ 8 Sentosa Gateway
▪ 6577-8888 ▪ Open 10am–
7pm daily ▪ Adm ▪ www.
rwsentosa.com

The biggest draw on Sentosa,
this movie-centric theme
park has many high-octane
rides, Hollywood-style film
sets, and more.

③ The Far East Organization's Children's Garden

Open 9am–7pm Tue–Sun,
last adm 6pm (water play
area closes 6:30pm)

This watery fun garden at Gardens
by the Bay is a free attraction that is
perfect for kids. It has an
obstacle adventure trail,
treehouses, a toddlers'
play zone, and inter-
active water features.
A family-friendly café
is on site, too.

④ Science Centre Singapore

MAP R2 ▪ 15 Science
Centre Rd ▪ 6425-2500
▪ Open 10am–6pm daily
(observatory: open
7–10pm Fri) ▪ Adm
▪ www.science.edu.sg

The largely interactive
exhibits at this remark-
able science museum
challenge kids to take
on subjects as diverse
as climate change,
optics, ageing, and robotics.

⑤ Singapore Discovery Centre

MAP Q2 ▪ 510 Upper Jurong Rd
▪ 6792-6188 ▪ Open noon–7pm
Mon–Fri, 11am–8pm Sat, Sun & hols
▪ Adm ▪ www.sdc.com.sg

This museum, in the west of
Singapore, features a variety
of interactive exhibits,
augmented reality games,
and activities for visitors
to immerse themselves
into Singapore's past,
present, and future.

⑥ Snow City

MAP R2 ▪ 21 Jurong
Town Hall Rd ▪ 6560-2306
▪ Open 10am–6pm daily
(last adm 5pm) ▪ Adm
▪ www.snowcity.com.sg

Snowman at Snow City

Snow City brings the Arctic
to the tropics, with igloos,
sub-zero temperatures,
and simulated snowfall.
There are also bumper cars and
a climbing wall. Warm coats
and boots are provided.

7 Jurong Bird Park

This is one of the largest parks of its kind *(see p101)*. A suspended bridge runs through the Waterfall Aviary, featuring the world's tallest artificial waterfall.

8 Adventure Cove Waterpark

MAP S3 ■ 8 Sentosa Gateway ■ 6577-8888 ■ Open 10am–6pm daily ■ Adm ■ www.rwsentosa.com

High-speed water slides, snorkeling above a tropical reef, and tubing down Adventure River are among the attractions here.

9 SuperPark

MAP N1 ■ #02–477 Suntec City Tower 1, 3 Temasek Boulevard ■ 6239-5360 ■ Open 10:30am–8pm Mon–Fri, 9am–9pm Sat, Sun & hols ■ Adm ■ www.superpark.com.sg

This indoor play park has something for kids and adults alike. Activities include pedal car racing, trampolining, wall climbing, and various obstacles.

10 S.E.A. Aquarium

MAP S3 ■ 8 Sentosa Gateway ■ 6577-8888 ■ Open 10am–6pm daily ■ Adm ■ www.rwsentosa.com

With nine different zones, including the Predators of the Sea, this aquarium mesmerizes everyone through close-up encounters with marine life.

Fish tank at S.E.A. Aquarium

TOP 10 OUTDOOR ACTIVITIES

Wakeboarding in Singapore

1 Sea Canoeing
Kayaks and canoes can be rented at the Sentosa Nature Park *(see p47)*.

2 Golf
MAP T3 ■ 80 Rhu Cross ■ 6345-7788
Just east of the center of the city, the 18-hole Marina Bay Golf Course is open to the public and has great views.

3 Wakeboarding
MAP U2 ■ 1206A East Coast Parkway ■ 6636-4266
The Singapore Wake Park tows wakeboarders around a cableway.

4 Windsurfing
MAP T3 ■ 1212 East Coast Parkway ■ 6241-9212
Aloha Sea Sports Centre offers both instruction and equipment.

5 Sailing
MAP U2 ■ 1500 East Coast Parkway ■ 6444-4555
The Singapore Sailing Federation runs courses for all ages.

6 Swimming
MAP T2 ■ 100 Tyrwhitt Rd ■ 6293-9058
The Jalan Besar Swimming Complex is the most centrally located of the island's numerous Olympic-sized pools, with only nominal admission fees.

7 Hiking
Hike through rainforest at Bukit Timah *(see p102)* and MacRitchie *(see p47)*.

8 Biking
Rent bikes at East Coast Park *(see p47)*, Sentosa, and Pulau Ubin *(see p51)*.

9 Rollerblading
East Coast Park is superb for rollerblading, and has several rental shops.

10 Beach Volleyball
Siloso Beach *(see pp32–3)* has four popular courts, so go early at weekends.

🔟 Arts Venues

An exhibit at NUS Museum

① NUS Museum
50 Kent Ridge Crescent, National University of Singapore ■ 6516-8817 ■ Open 10am–6pm Tue–Sat ■ www.museum.nus.edu.sg

The university's museum displays Southeast Asian and Chinese art, including brush paintings and porcelain. It also hosts exhibitions of modern art, a constant fixture being sculptures and ceramics by a home-grown modern master, Ng Eng Teng.

② Singapore Art Museum (SAM)
MAP M1 ■ 71 Bras Basah Rd ■ www.singaporeartmuseum.sg

Known for its collections of local and Southeast Asian art, SAM predates the more famous National Gallery. It is undergoing a major renovation, but exhibitions are being organized at partner venues. The building is scheduled to reopen in 2026.

③ STPI – Creative Workshop & Gallery
MAP J2 ■ 41 Robertson Quay ■ 6336-3663 ■ Open 10am–7pm Mon–Fri (until 5pm Sun), 9am–6pm Sat ■ www.stpi.com.sg

Established in 2002, this institute works with international artists to create outstanding prints and explore the technical and creative aspects of print and paper-making. It is housed in a 19th-century warehouse where artists create, exhibit, and sell work.

④ Gillman Barracks
MAP S3 ■ 9 Lock Rd ■ Open Tue–Sun ■ www.gillmanbarracks.com

Occupying a former British army barracks built in 1936, this cluster of galleries showcases modern Southeast Asian and international artists. The on-site Centre for NTU Contemporary Art also offers exhibitions and lectures.

⑤ The Esplanade – Theatres on the Bay

This iconic landmark of Singapore, built as a center for the performing arts (see p42), houses two indoor stages (a concert hall and a smaller recital studio) for music, theater, and dance performances by international and local groups. There is an outdoor stage beside Marina Bay.

The Esplanade – Theatres on the Bay

8 National Gallery Singapore

A lavish bid to create a world-class art museum, the National Gallery (see p40) displays Singaporean and Malayan art in its City Hall wing, plus works from elsewhere in Southeast Asia in the former Supreme Court. There are regular talks, workshops, volunteer-led tours, and other events.

6 KC Arts Centre
MAP J2 ■ 20 Merbau Rd, Robertson Quay ■ 6221-5585 ■ www.srt.com.sg

Home to the award-winning Singapore Repertory Theatre – one of Asia's leading English-language theater companies – KC is located amid dining and nightlife venues. The Little Company hosts performances for children here.

7 The Arts House at Old Parliament House

Rooms that were once used for parliamentary discussions now welcome music and dance performances, poetry readings, lectures, screenings, and other fringe events. The old rooms are intimate, with hardwood floors, decorative molding, and special fixtures, all intact. The building (see p15) also has a restaurant.

National Gallery Singapore's terrace

9 The Substation
MAP L1 ■ 45 Armenian St ■ 6337-7535 ■ www.substation.org

Singapore's first home for the city's independent artists has a black box theater, a gallery, and multipurpose rooms. These host diverse events from indie gigs to film festivals.

10 Victoria Theatre and Concert Hall

Though home to the Singapore Symphony Orchestra, this concert hall (see p89) stages other performances as well. The details of this revamped, ornate building are as much a part of the performance as the music itself.

📘10 Bars and Lounges

SkyBar at CÉ LA VI has views across the Singapore skyline

1 CÉ LA VI
MAP N4 ▪ 1 Bayfront Ave, Sands SkyPark, Marina Bay Sands Tower 3 ▪ 6508-2188 ▪ Open noon–late daily

In a stunning location on top of Marina Bay Sands, this venue features the alfresco SkyBar. A multitiered restaurant serves Modern Asian cuisine, and there is also a chic nightclub.

2 Atlas Bar
MAP G5 ▪ Parkview Square, 600 North Bridge Rd ▪ 6396-4466 ▪ Open 10–1am Mon–Thu (until 2am Fri), noon–2am Sat

One of Singapore's most opulent bars, Atlas has 1920s-style decor that includes a large cabinet devoted to a collection of rare gins and champagnes. By day it's an informal place for a cocktail or coffee, but a smart casual dress code applies after 5pm.

3 Little Island Brewing Co.
MAP V1 ▪ 6 Changi Village Rd #01-01 ▪ 6543-9100 ▪ Open noon–midnight (from 11am Sat & Sun)

Located in Changi Village, this laid-back microbrewery serves a rotating selection of excellent in-house craft beers. It features alfresco seating areas where guests can gaze at the stars and enjoy the sea breeze.

Cocktail, Acid Bar

4 No. 5, Emerald Hill
MAP C5 ▪ 5 Emerald Hill Rd ▪ 6732-0818 ▪ Open noon–2am Mon–Thu (until 3am Fri & Sat), 2pm–2am Sun

In a restored 1910 Peranakan shophouse just off Orchard Road, No. 5 has a location, cocktail list, and buzzy ambience that all appeal to the expatriate crowd. In the day, it's quieter and easier to admire the Chinese teak carving and Peranakan decor.

5 Acid Bar
MAP C5 ▪ Peranakan Place, 180 Orchard Rd ▪ 6738-8828 ▪ Open 3pm–1am Mon–Thu, noon–2am Fri & Sat (until 1am Sun) ▪ No cover charge

The central location draws in crowds for live music, and the dance floor stays rowdy until late. Weekdays are more relaxed, with happy-hour drinks.

6 Smoke and Mirrors
MAP M2 ▪ #06-01 National Gallery, 1 St Andrew's Rd ▪ 9380-6313 ▪ Open 3pm–1am Mon–Thu (until 2am Fri), noon–2am Sat (until 1am Sun)

Offering splendid views over the Padang, with Marina Bay Sands, Esplanade – Theatres By The Bay and the Singapore Flyer beyond, Smoke and Mirrors offers a wide range of cocktails as well as snacks.

7 Alley Bar
MAP C5 ■ 2 Emerald Hill Rd
■ 6738-8818 ■ Open 5pm–2am daily

Tucked between two heritage Peranakan shophouses, this elegant cocktail bar serves innovative drinks inspired by the local flavors and history of Singapore.

8 Mama Diam
MAP F5 ■ 38 Prinsep St #01-01 ■ 8533-0792 ■ Open 4–10:30pm daily

Slide open the magazine rack at a seemingly dime-a-dozen sundries shop (locally known as a mama shop) to find this modern speakeasy. The outdoor area has vintage knick-knacks and an easy-going, old-school feel. Its menu features Southeast Asian-inspired cocktails.

Bar counter at Harry's

9 Harry's, Boat Quay
MAP L3 ■ 28 Boat Quay ■ 6532-5828 ■ Open 11:30am–midnight Sun–Thu (until 1am Fri & Sat)

Popular with tourists and banking executives, this riverside bar has alfresco seating and live sports.

10 MO Bar
MAP N2 ■ Mandarin Oriental, 5 Raffles Ave ■ 6885-3500 ■ Open 3pm–2am (from noon Sat & Sun)

Set on the fourth floor of the Mandarin Oriental hotel, this bar features floor-to-ceiling windows overlooking Marina Bay. It is the perfect place to have a drink while watching the city lights sparkle. The menu offers bespoke cocktails and beverages.

TOP 10 LOCAL DRINKS

1 Kopi
Made with Robusta beans that are wok-roasted with butter then strained through a sock after brewing, this local coffee has a distinct, earthy taste.

2 Lime Juice
This sweet and sour drink is made with calamansi limes native to Southeast Asia. Served cold, it is perfect for a hot day.

3 Teh Tarik
Tarik is Malay for "pull", and this milky tea is dramatically poured and "pulled" between two cups during its preparation to give it a frothy foam.

4 Milo Dinosaur
This sweet, iced chocolate drink topped with an extra scoop of Milo chocolate malt powder is a favorite with kids.

5 Bandung
A distinctive pink hue makes this fragrant condensed milk-and-rose syrup quencher stand out.

6 Chin Chow
An acquired taste, this cooling drink includes grass jelly "worms". It is believed to bring down fevers and lower high blood pressure.

7 Bubble Tea
This Taiwanese drink is popular with younger Singaporeans. The chewy tapioca pearls in the sweet tea are addictive.

8 Sugarcane Juice
Part of the fun of ordering this drink is watching the drinks seller put the long canes through the hand-cranked juice extractor.

9 Barley Water
Said to cool one's "internal fire", this traditional Chinese drink is made with barley pearls simmered in water until soft, then sweetened with rock sugar or candied winter melon.

10 Singapore Sling
This fruity, gin-based cocktail was invented in 1915 at the Long Bar in the Raffles Hotel *(see p30)*.

🔟 Restaurants

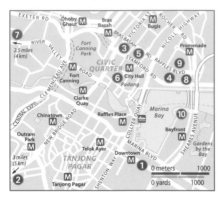

Artistically presented, the refined seasonal menus look as beautiful as they taste.

4 Morton's The Steakhouse
Ebullient waiters at this upmarket steak-house *(see p93)* follow the menu with an immense platter, heaving with sample cuts of beef or vegetables. The seafood competes with superbly fresh lobsters, oysters, and shrimp. Try the Chicago-style prime bone-in ribeye or the Maine lobster cocktail. The modern interiors, bright decor and excellent food make this a must visit.

5 Mikuni
With a modern approach to Japanese cuisine, Mikuni *(see p93)* offers a *robatayaki* grilling counter, and live teppanyaki as well as sushi stations, each headed by a master chef. The cuisine highlights Japanese seasonal produce and offers a multi-sensory dining experience.There are also set menus for lunch and dinner, and select beers and wines. Reserve a table in advance.

1 Majestic Restaurant
Established in 2006, this stylish restaurant *(see p93)* located right in the heart of Marina Bay's banking district serves beautifully presented, modern Cantonese dishes. It is helmed by the award-winning chef, Yong Bing Ngen. Specialties include Chinese-style honey lamb chops and noodles with Boston lobster.

2 TungLok Heen
The perfect retreat for those who appreciate traditional and delicious Chinese cuisine *(see p105)*. The menu includes an array of fresh Teochew delights and fiery Hunan cuisine besides celebrity chef Susur Lee's signature creations, such as roast Irish duck. The interiors feature elegant wood accents and perfectly complement the food.

3 Whitegrass
MAP M1 ■ #01-26 CHIJMES, 30 Victoria St ■ 6837-0402 ■ Open noon–2:30pm & 6–10:30pm Tue–Sat ■ www.whitegrass.com.sg ■ $$$
Housed within the spruce grounds of a former Catholic convent, chef Takuya Yamashita's Michelin-starred restaurant showcases classical French fare with a Japanese touch.

The lively sushi station at Mikuni

The Ritz-Carlton's Summer Pavilion, offering fine Cantonese cuisine

6 National Kitchen by Violet Oon

Opened in 2015, this acclaimed restaurant enjoys a great location at the National Gallery of Singapore. Here, guests can try a selection of classic Singapore dishes *(see p93)*, drawing on Peranakan cuisine, street food as well as Chinese, Malay and Indian traditions, put together by one of the country's veteran chefs.

7 Candlenut

The world's first Michelin-starred Peranakan restaurant, Candlenut *(see p105)* takes a modern yet traditional approach to Straits-Chinese cuisine. Chef Malcolm Lee's must-try creative dishes include *kueh pie tee* (crispy pastry cups) with blue swimmer crab and turmeric curry.

Kueh pie tee, a spicy sweet tart

8 Summer Pavilion

Awarded with the Michelin star four times, the Ritz-Carlton's swankiest restaurant *(see p93)* serves top-class Cantonese food in an elegant Chinese garden setting.

The dim sum and lobster noodles are extremely popular. Set lunches are good value. Do try the range of teas as well.

9 Rang Mahal

In business since 1971, this restaurant is renowned for its pursuit of excellence. Expect a range of cuisines from the northern, coastal, and southern regions of India, all complemented by an expansive wine list. For guests visiting on a Sunday, Rang Mahal *(see p93)* offers a gourmet lunch buffet featuring live cooking stations and a range of desserts.

10 CUT

Celebrity chef Wolfgang Puck's first Asian venture *(see p93)* puts a contemporary twist on the classic steakhouse menu. The modern interiors, by award-winning designer Tony Chi, complement the delectable cuisine at this Michelin-starred restaurant. Along with the finest cuts of beef, diners will find a fabulous wine cellar with more than 500 options, a cocktail menu, and impeccable service here.

For a key to restaurant price ranges see p77

🔟 Hawker Centers and Food Courts

A stall at Maxwell Food Centre

1 Maxwell Food Centre
MAP K5 ▪ Corner of South Bridge Rd & Maxwell Rd ▪ Open 8–2am daily

A Chinatown favorite, this hawker center has an extensive menu of Chinese favorites, usually served with rice. Try the famous Hainanese chicken at Tian Tian Hainanese Chicken Rice stall.

2 East Coast Lagoon Food Village
MAP U2 ▪ 1220 East Coast Park Service Rd ▪ Open 11am–11pm daily

Ocean breezes keep eating areas cool at this center beside the sea. Find good barbecued seafood at Leng Heng, oyster omeletes at Song Kee, and satay at Haron 55.

The East Coast Lagoon Food Village

3 Tiong Bahru Food Centre
MAP T3 ▪ 83 Seng Poh Rd ▪ Open 6am–11pm daily

Located in hip Tiong Bahru, one of Singapore's oldest public housing estates, this spot has more than 80 stalls. The emphasis is on Chinese fare such as Hainanese chicken rice, roast pork, and fishball noodles. Note that the center is usually very busy.

4 Newton Food Centre
MAP C2 ▪ 500 Clemenceau Ave North ▪ Open noon–2am daily

Established in the 1970s, this old-school, open-air food court draws tourists in large numbers. Food here can be pricier than average and the seafood is sold by weight. Most stalls open only in the late afternoon.

5 Satay by the Bay
MAP P4 ▪ 18 Marina Gardens Drive ▪ Open 11am–10pm daily

A pair of satay stalls do a roaring trade at this open-air food court in Gardens by the Bay (pp28–9). Claypot rice and the dishes at Boon Tat Street Barbecued Seafood are popular choices.

6 Tekka Market
MAP F3 ▪ 665 Buffalo Rd ▪ Open 8am–11pm daily

This popular hawker center is good for local Indian fare such as spicy

fried noodles, fish-head curry, and *rojak* (fritters with a sweet chili dip). Also here is one of Singapore's largest wet markets. Busiest in the morning, it sells meat, seafood, vegetables, and tropical fruit.

7 Food Republic
Wisma Atria: MAP B4; 435 Orchard Rd ▪ Suntec City Mall: MAP P2; Temasek Ave ▪ VivoCity: MAP S3

This mall food court chain offers a slick take on the traditional hawker center. The VivoCity outlet has the look of a village from yesteryear.

Lau Pa Sat Festival Market

8 Lau Pa Sat Festival Market
MAP M4 ▪ 18 Raffles Quay ▪ Open 11–3am daily

In the heart of the banking district this hawker center features Victorian cast-iron architecture and a good range of stalls. It is usually packed at lunchtime, in the evening, satay stalls outside are worth a visit.

9 Chinatown Complex
MAP K4 ▪ Block 335 Smith St ▪ Open 11am–11pm daily

Known for Chinese food, this hawker center has offerings such as local-style savory carrot cake, claypot rice, and dumplings.

10 Makansutra Glutton's Bay
MAP N2 ▪ 8 Raffles Ave ▪ Open 6pm–3am daily

Good for late snacking, this very popular waterfront place offers a reasonable selection of food, including barbecued chicken wings.

TOP 10 LOCAL DISHES

Chicken satay and peanut sauce

1 Satay
These are small skewers of barbecued meats – chicken, beef, mutton – dipped in a sweet peanut and chili sauce.

2 Kaya Toast
A sweet jam made from coconut milk and egg is spread on toast and eaten for breakfast or as a snack.

3 Chili Crab
Whole crab smothered in a sweet and sour, spicy sauce, served with buns for dipping in the sauce.

4 Fish Head Curry
An entire fish head stewed in spicy curry – the cheek meat is said to be the sweetest of the whole animal.

5 Banana Leaf Rice
Southern Indian meal of white rice, vegetable curries, and relish served on a flat banana leaf.

6 Nasi Padang
Indonesian or Malay cooked dishes, such as beef *rendang* or *assam* (tamarind) fish, served over white rice.

7 Laksa
Rice noodles, prawns, and fishcakes come together in a rich soup made from coconut curry, topped with chili and laksa leaf – a local herb.

8 Chicken Rice
Poached or roasted, chopped chicken served over rice that has been cooked in chicken stock.

9 Roti Prata
Indian griddle bread, sometimes containing egg, onion, or even cheese, and served with a curry dip.

10 Chendol
Dessert made of green jelly noodles, sweet beans, brown sugar, coconut milk, and shaved ice.

📖10 Shopping Malls

1 VivoCity
MAP S3 ▪ 1 Harbourfront Walk ▪ 6377-6860 ▪ Open 10am–10pm daily

Located on the waterfront, this mall has some of the city's best views, with platforms overlooking the cable cars swinging over to Sentosa. VivoCity is well designed and airy with great facilities, including food courts and restaurants, a multiplex cinema, and a children's playground.

Outdoor plaza at Ngee Ann City

2 Ngee Ann City
This marble monolith (see p95) is often known by the name of its main tenant, Takashimaya. The Japanese store rubs shoulders with luxury names, such as Louis Vuitton, Chanel. Fashion clothing chains include Zara and Dior. Bibliophiles should be sure to visit Kinokuniya (see p98), Singapore's largest bookstore.

3 Tanglin Shopping Centre
MAP A4 ▪ 19 Tanglin Rd ▪ 6737-0849 ▪ Open 10am–10pm daily

Not to be confused with Tanglin Mall, this place is a chance to escape familiar global brands and browse antiques, jewelry, and art in a relaxed atmosphere. The old-fashioned mall has a fine selection of traditional and modern Asian furniture, as well as hand-woven carpets and Middle Eastern collectables.

The Shoppes at Marina Bay Sands

4 Plaza Singapura
MAP E5 ▪ 68 Orchard Rd ▪ Open 10am–10pm daily

Plaza Singapura has stood the test of time, and remains popular by offering a wide range of good-value products, including clothing, musical instruments, and household items. There's a Marks & Spencer department store and many restaurants.

5 Funan
After its makeover in 2019, indoor cycling paths, a rooftop garden, a multiplex cinema, and a host of stylish serviced apartments were added to this mall complex (see p92). It features various food and beverage outlets, plus a good range of stores selling cameras, computers, and other electronic equipment.

6 The Shoppes at Marina Bay Sands
MAP N4 ▪ 10 Bayfront Ave ▪ 6688-8868 ▪ Open 10:30am–11pm Sun–Thu, 10:30am–11:30pm Fri–Sat

This vast luxury mall has over 300 stores featuring all the high-end designers. Sampans cruise along a canal at basement level, and there is an observation deck on the roof. Celebrity chef restaurants, trendy café-bars, and a food court provide a break from shopping.

Paragon shopping center

7 Paragon
MAP C4 ∎ 290 Orchard Rd ∎ 6738-5535 ∎ Open 10am–10pm daily

Exclusivity is the name of the game on Paragon's glamorous ground level, where designer boutiques such as Balenciaga, Prada, and Armani are located. The five other floors have more mainstream designers.

8 Jewel Changi Airport
MAP V2 ∎ 78 Airport Boulevard ∎ 6956-9898 ∎ Open 24 hours daily

This gleaming, ten-floor retail and entertainment complex is linked to three of the airport's passenger terminals. Its centerpiece is the world's tallest indoor waterfall, set amid a terraced forest.

9 Raffles City Shopping Centre
MAP M2 ∎ 252 North Bridge Rd ∎ 6318-0238 ∎ Open 10am–10pm daily

This center of interlinking malls joins the Stamford and Fairmont hotels with City Hall MRT, the CityLink, and Marina Square. It's home to a range of shops and eating places to suit all budgets.

10 ION Orchard
MAP B4 ∎ 2 Orchard Turn ∎ 6238-8228 ∎ Open 10am–10pm daily

You'll find dozens of high-end fashion and accessories shops, an art gallery, and a basement food hall at this high-rise mall, along with an observation deck (adm) that has panoramic views.

TOP 10 LOCAL BUYS

1 Jade
For fixed prices on luminescent green jade jewellery, head to Yue Hwa Chinese Emporium *(see p76)*.

2 Bak kwa
Chewy marinated barbecued pork slices, this portable snack is easily available throughout Chinatown.

3 Chinese Tea
Tea Chapter: 9 Neil Rd ∎ 6226-1175 ∎ Open 10:30am–9pm Sun–Thu (until 10:30pm Fri & Sat) ∎ www.teachapter.com
Quality teas packaged in attractive tins can be found on Neil Road.

4 Asian Art and Antiques
Best sourced at Tanglin Shopping Centre or Dempsey Hill.

5 Laksa Paste
This is the base for traditionally cooked laksa soup *(see p61)*.

6 Peranakan Porcelain
Rumah Bebe: 113 East Coast Rd ∎ 6247-8781 ∎ Open 11:30am–6:30pm Tue–Sun ∎ www.rumahbebe.com
Plates, tea sets, and spoons in various vibrant floral designs.

7 Tiger Balm
Formulated in the 1870s, this herbal ointment soothes aches and repels mosquitoes. Available at pharmacies.

8 Chinese Seals
Hand-carved personalised Chinese "chops" (seals) in various materials are easy to find in Chinatown's shops.

9 Kaya
Recreate kaya toast, the national breakfast, with a jar of this jam.

10 Batik
Sarongs, shirts, and fabrics with Malay and Indonesian designs are best bought in Kampong Glam.

Batik sarong designs

🔟 Singapore for Free

The Garden Rhapsody sound-and-light show at the Gardens by the Bay

1 Spectra Light and Sound Show

MAP N4 ■ Marina Bay Sands ■ Shows at 8 & 9pm daily (and 10pm Fri & Sat) ■ www.marinabaysands. com/attractions/spectra.html

Every evening, shows mesmerize viewers at Marina Bay Sands with orchestral music, multicolored strobes, and lovely choreographed fountains. The lights can sometimes be seen from a short distance as well.

2 Esplanade – Theatres on the Bay

There are often storytelling sessions, free concerts, and other activities here, some taking place at the waterfront Outdoor Stage (see p42). The Beautiful Sunday series, held once a month, show-cases local music groups in the spectacular Concert Hall. Exhibition spaces, the library, rooftop terrace, and children's PLAYbox are also freely accessible.

3 Student Concerts

MAP S2 ■ Yong Siew Toh Conservatory of Music, 3 Conservatory Drive ■ 6516-1167 ■ www.ystmusic.nus.edu.sg

Music students at the National University of Singapore stage free recitals here and at a few other venues, often during lunch hours.

4 Gardens by the Bay

Although there's a charge to enter the conservatories and SkyWalk, the rest of these world-famous gardens are free (see p28). Each night the music-and-light Garden Rhapsody show at the Supertree Grove wows visitors. This spectacular show is held at 7:45pm and 8:45pm

5 Sikh Gurdwaras

The British East India Company recruited Sikh *sepoys* to Singapore to be policemen in the 1800s, and the community now numbers around 13,000. In keeping with the Sikh inclusive ideology, visitors are welcomed at the seven *gurdwaras* (temples) in the city. Volunteer staff might offer tours, and the *langars* (communal kitchens) serve free, simple food and masala tea to all.

6 Art Tours

The 12 galleries at Gillman Barracks (see p54) are free to explore, and once a month you can register for a free art, history, and heritage tour of the colonial site. Some hotels, including Marina Bay Sands, the Hilton, and Pan Pacific, also have art collections in their public areas.

7 Concerts in the Park
www.nparks.gov.sg/sbg/
whats-happening/calendar-of-events
Free concerts are hosted in parks and
gardens across the city. The premier
spot is the Symphony Stage in the
Botanic Gardens. You may catch the
Singapore Symphony Orchestra or
an international act here.

8 Haw Par Villa
MAP S3 ■ 262 Pasir Panjang Rd
■ 6773-0103 ■ Open 9am–8pm daily
(until 10pm Fri & Sat) ■ www.hawpar
villa.sg
This Chinese folklore-themed park,
featuring grottoes depicting fantastical
scenes, was created by the family
behind Tiger Balm (see p63). Although
the Hell's Museum charges an admission fee, the gardens remain free.

The stunning Haw Par Villa complex

9 Hay Dairies
MAP R1 ■ 3 Lim Chu Kang
Lane 4 ■ 6792 0931 ■ Open 9am–4pm
Wed–Mon ■ www.haydairies.sg
There is no charge to visit this small
dairy farm, where you can pet the
goats. Visiting at milking time is
best, from 9am to 10:30am. It is in the
Kranji countryside, where many agri-
businesses and farms can be visited –
all connected by a bus service.

10 National Library
MAP M1 ■ 100 Victoria St
■ Open 10am–9pm daily ■ www.nlb.
gov.sg
The gleaming 16-floor central library
is an award-winning example of
"green" architecture. Regularly
changing art, photography, and
cultural exhibitions are free to visit.

TOP 10 BUDGET TIPS

1 Hawker Centers
Pick up dishes for as little as S$2 along
with the cheapest beers in town.

2 River Taxis
EZ-Link cards allow travel on "commuter"
bumboats for S$5 without paying for a
tour (www.rivercruise.com.sg).

3 Set Lunch Deals
Many restaurants have good-value set
lunch menus. Look out for all-you-can-
eat buffets too.

4 Cheap Nights Out
Most bars have daily happy hours with
"house pours", while some clubs also
have regular Ladies' Nights.

5 Eat Local
Generally, local and Asian cuisine is
cheaper than comparable Western meals.

6 Shopping Sales
The Great Singapore Sale takes place
every June through mid-August.

7 Walking Tours
There are free weekend walking tours
at the Botanic Gardens. Similar tours are
run at National Parks sites such as Bukit
Timah and Sungei Buloh. Advance registration is required (www.nparks.gov.sg).

8 Free Events
Besides religious and cultural festivals,
the city holds free arts performances,
live music, and museum talks (www.
peatix.com; www.eventbrite.sg).

9 The Singapore Pass
Save up to 57 per cent on attractions
and get free travel on hop-on hop-off
buses with some passes (www.hippo
pass.com/singapore).

10 Hop On Hop Off Buses
A fun way to see the city is through
companies that operate hop-on
hop-off bus tours (see p112).

Hop-on hop-off tour bus

🔟 Religious Celebrations

1 Chinese New Year
January or February

Singapore's most important public holiday is celebrated in January or February. Celebrations begin on the eve of the holiday, with families gathering for dinner. People visit friends and family, and *hong bao* (red packets containing money) are given to kids.

Chinese New Year decorations

Performers at Chingay Parade

2 Chingay Parade
January or February

This ticketed Chinese New Year parade features dance, music, and acrobatics as well as floats. More than 10,000 people take part, with troupes from all over the world adding a multicultural aspect.

3 Thaipusam
January or February

In January or February, this day of thanksgiving sees Hindus honor Lord Murugan. A parade begins at Sri Srinivasa Perumal Temple *(see p79)* and ends at Sri Thendayuthapani Temple *(see p38)*. Many devotees carry heavy *kavadis* (metal racks with fruits and flowers), pierce their tongues and cheeks, and dig hooks into their backs.

4 Hungry Ghost Festival
July or August

The Chinese believe that spirits wander the earth during the seventh month of the lunar calendar. To appease these hungry ghosts, they offer food, burn joss sticks and "hell money," and stage Chinese operas. New ventures, such as marriages and business openings, are discouraged during this inauspicious time.

5 Mid-Autumn Festival
September or October

Also called the Lantern Festival, this event celebrates the harvest with mooncakes stuffed with sweet lotus paste, egg yolks, and other fillings.

Mid-Autumn Festival celebrations

6 Hari Raya Puasa

Ramadan, the Muslim month of fasting, culminates with Hari Raya Puasa, and is celebrated with family and friends. Non-Muslims are often invited to feasts in private homes. The dates change every year.

Preparing the fire-walk for Thimithi

7 Thimithi
October or November

Each year, in October or November, a procession of Hindus makes its way from Little India's Sri Srinivasa Perumal Temple to the Sri Mariamman Temple (see p71).

8 Deepavali (Diwali)
October or November

This Hindu festival marks the triumph of good over evil. Hundreds of oil lamps are lit to guide the souls of the departed back to the afterlife.

9 Nine Emperor Gods
October

Taoists believe that the Nine Emperor Gods visit earth for nine days in November to care for the sick and bring luck to the living. Priests in Chinese temples chant, and spirit guides write charms in blood.

10 Christmas
December

The city keeps the Christmas spirit alive with spectacular decorations along Orchard Road (see pp94–9).

TOP 10 SPORTING AND CULTURAL EVENTS

1 Singapore Art Week
Visual art comes to the fore every January with two weeks of special art talks, exhibition launches, and the like.

2 World Gourmet Summit
August sees Singapore host a festival of fine dining, with demonstrations by international celebrity chefs.

3 Dragon Boat Festival
International teams race dragon boats at the Marina Bay in June.

4 Great Singapore Sale
For six weeks in June and July, local retailers offer excellent discounts.

5 Singapore Food Festival
This month-long celebration of local food, including tours and classes, is held across the city every July.

6 Ballet Under the Stars
This casual event is held at various outdoor venues across the city every July. Perfect for a cultural evening.

7 Singapore International Festival of the Arts
This annual arts festival, held mostly in May and June, draws performers from around the world and spans genres such as theater, dance, and music.

8 National Day, August 9
A huge show marks the day Singapore became a nation. Tickets are only available via a public lottery.

9 Formula 1 Singapore Grand Prix
Held each year in September, this is the first night time race in Grand Prix history and Asia's first to be held on city streets.

10 Singapore International Film Festival
Some 300 independent films are shown in November and December, with a special focus on Asian cinema.

National Day, August 9

Singapore
Area by Area

The stunning Chinatown
cityscape at night

TOP10 Chinatown

In 1822, Sir Stamford Raffles laid out a plan that divided Singapore into clearly defined quarters. At the time, the area south of the Singapore River was developing fast, with godowns (warehouses) and shipping offices opening up, and Chinese laborers living in cramped conditions behind them. Chinese temples sprang up alongside clan associations: groups of Chinese who had a common dialect, name, or similar origins. Indian workers also lived here, especially after the opening of the port at Tanjong Pagar in the mid-1800s. Taoist and Hindu temples, churches, and mosques stand side by side, typifying the multicultural spirit of the city.

Buddha Tooth Relic Temple

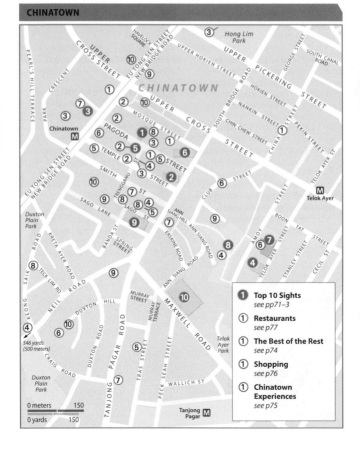

CHINATOWN

1	**Top 10 Sights** see pp71–3
1	**Restaurants** see p77
1	**The Best of the Rest** see p74
1	**Shopping** see p76
1	**Chinatown Experiences** see p75

Chinatown Heritage Centre exhibit

① Chinatown Heritage Centre

MAP K4 ■ 48 Pagoda St ■ 6224-3928 ■ Open 9:30am–6pm daily ■ www.chinatown.sg ■ Adm

This museum, located in three restored shophouses in the heart of Chinatown, illustrates the harsh conditions in which the Chinese community lived and worked in Singapore's early days. Occupying three levels, it re-creates scenes from old shops, coffee shops, and living cubicles, with an interesting exhibit dedicated to the "four evils" of gambling, opium smoking, prostitution, and secret societies.

② Sri Mariamman Temple

MAP K4 ■ 244 South Bridge Rd ■ 6223-4064 ■ Open 7am–noon & 6–9pm daily ■ www.smt.org.sg

Sri Mariamman, or "Mother Goddess" as she is known to Hindus, is honored at this temple, Singapore's oldest Hindu place of worship. It was established in 1827 by Narayana Pillay, a government clerk who arrived aboard Raffles' ship. The current temple was built in 1843 by former Indian convicts. The goddess, Sri Mariamman, is believed to cure diseases.

③ People's Park Complex

MAP K4 ■ 1 Park Rd ■ Open 8am–late daily ■ www.peoplesparkcomplex.com

This towering concrete block was a ground-breaking development – an emblem of Asian Modernism – when it was built in the 1970s. The central mall is thick with travel agents, electronics shops, Chinese souvenirs, massage specialists, and beauty therapists. Spilling out at ground level around the mall are kiosks selling local snacks and money changers offering decent rates. The adjacent People's Park Complex Food Centre has dozens of hawker stands, and is justifiably packed day and night.

④ Al-Abrar Mosque

MAP L5 ■ 192 Telok Ayer St ■ 6220-6306 ■ Open 11:30am–9pm Sat–Thu, 10am–9pm Fri

Once the island's most important mosque, Al-Abrar was originally a seaside hut built from wood and *attap* (palm thatch). It served the community living and working in the area – hence its name "Kuchu Palli," or "small hut house." Squeezed between shophouses, with its facade blending in with the city, it is very quiet. It serves Chinatown workers, as most Muslims prefer to pray at mosques closer to home.

Sri Mariamman Temple exterior

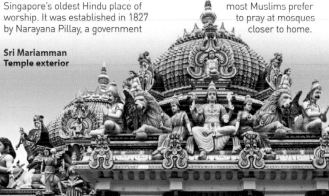

Visitors throng the food stalls and shops of the Chinatown Street Market

⑤ Chinatown Street Market

MAP K4 ■ Trengganu St & Pagoda St ■ Open 10am–11pm daily

Closed to vehicles, these two streets are lined with stalls selling a jumble of gifts and trinkets, mainly from China. There are also batiks and carved wood items, most likely from Indonesia, and lacquerware and silk items from Vietnam. Behind the stalls, stores sell pricier gifts, art, and antiques. Nearby Smith Street is also partly closed to traffic, as food is served from roadside stalls.

⑥ Jamae (Chulia) Mosque

MAP K4 ■ 218 South Bridge Rd ■ 6221-4165 ■ Open 10am–6pm daily; closed noon–2:30pm Fri ■ www.masjidjamaechulia.sg

The Chulias were Muslims who were engaged in trade and money-changing and who came from India's southern coast. They financed the building of the nearby Al-Abrar Mosque as well as this. Its impressive facade is southern Indian in style, with latticework embellishment and two tall minarets with *mihrabs* (small niches) carved in the sides. Cloaks are available inside the entrance for visitors wearing shorts or sleeveless tops.

⑦ Thian Hock Keng Temple

Though a main stop on every tourist itinerary, Thian Hock Keng *(see pp16–17)* maintains its charm. Built in the architectural style of southern Chinese temples, it follows *feng shui*, traditional rules that govern the placement of objects for optimal flow of energy. Though Taoist and dedicated to the goddess Ma Zu (Ma Cho Po), it respects Buddhist teachings, too, with a shrine of Bodhisattva Guanyin and the Buddhist swastika embellishing its walls.

⑧ Ann Siang Hill Park

MAP K4, L4 ■ Park entrances: Amoy St & Club St

Chinatown and Tanjong Pagar were once covered in hills, but most have been levelled. Ann Siang Hill is one of the few that remains. This park stretches along the hilltop, with stairs and boardwalks offering views over shophouse rooftops.

Jamae (Chulia) Mosque minarets

9 Buddha Tooth Relic Temple

MAP K4 ■ 288 South Bridge Rd ■ 6220-0220 ■ Open 7am–7pm daily ■ www.btrts.org.sg

This complex, completed in 2007 at a cost of S$53 million, houses a sacred tooth relic of the Buddha. The building contains halls for prayer and meditation, a theater, museums, an exhibition center, a gift shop, and a teahouse. While the layout is based on the Buddhist order of the cosmos, the architecture is inspired by the Tang Dynasty of China. Shorts, skirts, and sleeveless tops are not allowed.

Icon, Buddha Tooth Relic Temple

10 Singapore City Gallery

MAP K5 ■ 43 Maxwell Rd ■ 6221-6666 ■ Open 9am–5pm Mon–Sat ■ www.ura.gov.sg

Housed at the Urban Redevelopment Authority – Singapore's central planning agency – this gallery gives an overview of heritage conservation and future grand projects, aided by huge scale models of the island. Regular guided tours present the official view of what Singapore needs next.

CLANS AND ASSOCIATIONS

From the 1820s, as Chinese immigrants settled in the area south of the Singapore River, clans, associations, and temples sprang up to offer community support. Many of these groups are still housed in Chinatown's shophouses, and play an integral role in preserving the culture of Singapore's Chinese community.

A DAY IN CHINATOWN

▶ MORNING

From the Chinatown MRT, take the overhead walkway across Eu Tong Sen Street and New Bridge Road to Pagoda Street. Start the day here, at the **Chinatown Heritage Centre** (see p71), which will give you an overview of the neighborhood's rich history. Outside, meander past the stalls of the **Chinatown Street Market** at Pagoda and Trengganu streets, where shops sell drinks and snacks. Nearby, on South Bridge Road, shophouses, temples, and mosques stand side by side. Here, you can visit the **Jamae (Chulia) Mosque** on the corner of Mosque Street, the **Sri Mariamman Temple** (see p71), and the **Buddha Tooth Relic Temple**, situated on South Bridge Road.

AFTERNOON

Try some local dishes and have something cool to drink at one of the foodstalls at the **Maxwell Food Centre** (see p60) opposite the **Buddha Tooth Relic Temple**. If you prefer to eat lunch in a restaurant, stroll up Ann Siang Hill to Club Street, where you will find a selection of chic Asian and international restaurants in restored shophouses. After lunch, take a stroll along Club Street to admire the architecture, then take the shortcut through **Ann Siang Hill Park** to Amoy Street, where many legal, public relations, and advertising firms have offices. The park ends just behind the **Thian Hock Keng Temple** (see pp16–17).

See map on p70 ←

The Best of the Rest

1 Preserved Shophouses
MAP L4 ▪ China St

The pedestrianized streets either side of China Street contain rows of shophouses, converted into offices and restaurants as part of the China Square and Far East Square developments.

2 Bee Cheng Hiang
MAP K4 ▪ 189 New Bridge Rd
▪ 6223-7059 ▪ Open 8am–10pm daily

Specializing in *bak kwa* – slices of barbecued pork – in many flavors, Bee Cheng Hiang has lines going around the block in the holidays.

3 Speakers' Corner
MAP K3 ▪ Hong Lim Park, Upper Pickering St & New Bridge Rd ▪ Open 24 hours

This stage in a public park is the official platform for public speaking in Singapore. Protests and demonstrations are also held here.

4 Baba House
MAP T3 ▪ 157 Neil Rd
▪ 6227-5731 ▪ Advance booking required ▪ www.babahouse.nus.edu.sg

Dating to the 1890s, this indigo-blue Peranakan house offers free tours five times a week. Beautiful period features and original antiques reveal the life of a wealthy Straits-Chinese family 100 years ago.

5 Mei Heong Yuen Dessert
MAP K4 ▪ 63–7 Temple St
▪ 6221-1156 ▪ Open noon–9:30pm Tue–Sun

Enjoy Chinese desserts here. Try the almond, walnut, and sesame pastes or a Mango Snow Ice.

6 Club Street
MAP K4, L4

Once home to many Chinese clan associations, this lively street has boutiques, bars, and restaurants.

7 Tong Heng Confectionery
MAP K4 ▪ 285 South Bridge Rd
▪ 6223-3649 ▪ Open 9am–7pm daily

This lovely patisserie serves Chinese-style egg tarts, a local version of the very popular Portuguese recipe.

8 Tai Chong Kok
MAP K4 ▪ 34 Sago St
▪ 6226-3588 ▪ Open 9am–8pm daily (until 6:30pm Mon)

Traditionally filled with lotus seed paste, the modern mooncakes sold year-round come in many different flavors.

Mooncake, Tai Chong Kok

9 Chinese Weekly Entertainment Club
MAP K4 ▪ 76 Club St ▪ No public access

Built in 1891, this mansion was once a draw for Singapore's socialites. Now it is a secretive private members' club.

10 Duxton Hill
MAP K5

This small cluster of conservation shophouses is a charming retreat during the day, and it is then beautifully lit in the evenings, when drinkers and diners come to enjoy the eclectic restaurants and bars.

Shophouse facade, Duxton Hill

Chinatown Experiences

1 Chinatown Night Market
MAP K4 ■ Pagoda St

Watch sidewalk calligraphers translate foreign names into Chinese characters (see p76).

Chinatown Night Market calligrapher

2 Thye Shan Medical Hall
MAP K4 ■ 201 New Bridge Rd ■ 6223 1326 ■ Open 9:30am–8pm daily ■ www.thyeshan.com

A traditional, family-run Chinese medicine dispensary lined with shelves of glass jars and drawers containing fragrant fresh herbs.

3 Chinese Snacks
MAP K4 ■ People's Park Complex, 1 Park Rd

Kiosks and stalls here sell mainland Chinese snacks that are hard to find elsewhere, including pastries, sweet buns and savoury pancakes.

4 Chinese Theatre Circle
MAP K4 ■ 5 Smith St ■ 6323-4862 ■ Open noon–5pm Tue–Sat, 2–6pm Sun ■ www.ctcopera.com ■ Adm

There are karaoke-style Chinese opera shows in the afternoon followed by formal evening shows with meals on Fridays and Saturdays.

5 Food Playground
MAP K4 ■ 24A Sago St ■ 9452-3669 ■ www.foodplayground.com.sg

Home cooks teach guests about Singapore's street-food culture and how to prepare classic dishes.

6 Nanyin Music
MAP L4 ■ Thian Hock Keng Temple, 158 Telok Ayer St ■ www.siongleng.com

Every year, the temple hosts a handful of evening performances of traditional Chinese music in the southern *nanyin* style. The local Siong Leng organization runs this.

7 Nam's Supplies
MAP K4 ■ 22 Smith St ■ 6324-5872 ■ Open 8am–6pm daily

This store sells fake banknotes and paper replicas of luxury goods, or "hell money", burned to reach departed souls in the afterlife.

8 Chinese Chess
MAP K4 ■ Sago St & Trengganu St

Amid touristy shops, locals still gather to play chess.

9 The Tea Chapter
MAP K5 ■ 9 Neil Rd ■ 6226-1175 ■ Open 11am–9pm Sun–Thu (until 10:30pm Fri & Sat) ■ www.teachapter.com ■ Adm

Learn the art of the traditional Chinese tea ceremony while you relax in this teahouse.

10 Wet Market
MAP K4 ■ Chinatown Complex ■ Open 5am–noon Tue–Sun

The floors of this market are hosed with water daily. It sells fruit, vegetables, meats, and dried goods.

Fish stall at Chinatown's Wet Market

See map on p70

Shopping

1 Yue Hwa Chinese Emporium
MAP K4 ■ 70 Eu Tong Sen St ■ 6538-4222 ■ Open 11am–9pm daily (until 10pm Sat)

This emporium is recommended for its variety of Chinese handicrafts, from silk clothing to embroidered linen, jade jewelry, and gifts at affordable prices.

Chop, Chinatown Seal Carving

2 The Tintin Shop
MAP K4 ■ 28 Pagoda St ■ 8183-2210 ■ Open 10am–9pm daily

Fans of Belgian cartoonist Hergé's famous comic-book detective will find all sorts of Tintin-related merchandise at this store.

Display at The Tintin Shop

3 Da Wei Arts n Crafts
MAP K4 ■ 10 Trengganu St ■ 6224-5058 ■ Open 11am–10pm daily

This store stocks Chinese art supplies such as paper, ink, and brushes.

4 Zhen Lacquer Gallery
MAP K4 ■ 1 Trengganu St ■ 6222-2718 ■ Open 10:30am–9pm daily

This small, friendly shop specializes in lacquerware products, including some attractive bowls.

5 Orchid Chopsticks
MAP K4 ■ 65 Pagoda St ■ 6423-0488 ■ Open 10am–10pm daily

The ornamental and customized chopsticks sold here make wonderful small gifts for friends and family back home.

6 Chinatown Seal Carving
MAP K4 ■ #02–06 Lucky Chinatown, 211 New Bridge Rd ■ 9817-8781 ■ Open 11am–7pm daily

Craftsmen here will spell your name or chosen message in Chinese characters and carve it onto your choice of stone "chops" (Chinese stamps).

7 Poh Heng
MAP K4 ■ #01–17 People's Park Complex, 1 Park Rd ■ 6535-0960 ■ Open 11:30am–9pm daily

Specializing in gold and jade, this venerable jeweler also has some attractive Peranakan-style brooches.

8 Peranakan Tile Gallery
MAP K4 ■ 36 Temple St #01-04 ■ 6684-8600 ■ Open noon–6pm daily ■ www.asterbykyra.sg

This small shop sells ornate wall tiles that were once used to decorate Singapore's traditional shophouses.

9 Chinatown Complex
MAP K4 ■ Sago St & Trengganu St ■ Open 9am–9pm daily

This complex sells mostly household goods, but there are some unusual finds for the bargain hunter.

10 World Arts & Crafts
MAP K4 ■ #B1–28 People's Park Centre, 101 Upper Cross St ■ 6532-0056 ■ Open noon–7pm daily

With a collection from as far as China and South America, this store sells crystals set in jewelry as well as in their natural rock forms.

Restaurants

PRICE CATEGORIES

For a three-course meal for one with a non-alcoholic drink (or equivalent meal), taxes, and extra charges.
$ under S$30 $$ S$30–70 $$$ over S$70

1 Fortune Court
MAP K4 ■ 31 Pagoda St ■ 9234-9969 ■ Open 11am–3pm & 5:30–10pm daily ■ $$

This modern restaurant specializes in Cantonese cuisine served hot from the wok. Try the lobster in spicy XO sauce with *ee-fu* egg noodles, or the white pepper crab cooked seven ways.

2 Yum Cha
MAP K4 ■ 20 Trengganu St ■ 6372-1717 ■ Open 10:30am–10pm Mon–Fri (from 9am Sat & Sun) ■ $$

A popular old-style shophouse serving delicious, freshly made dim sum, Cantonese treats such as Peking duck, and crispy pastries.

3 Nomiya
MAP K4 ■ 11 Trengganu St ■ 6232-7827 ■ Open 11:30am–2:30pm & 5:30–10:30pm Tue–Sun ■ $$

Enjoy contemporary Japanese sharing plates accompanied by a fine selection of saké.

4 PS Café Ann Siang Hill
MAP K4 ■ 45 Ann Siang Rd, #02-02 ■ 6708-9288 ■ Open 11:30am–10pm daily ■ $$

Set in Ann Siang Hill Park, this bistro-style restaurant serves great drinks and modern interpretations of local flavors. Try the blue swimmer crab tart with chili and kaffir.

5 Cumi Bali
MAP K5 ■ 50 Tras St ■ 6220 6619 ■ Open 11:30am–3pm & 6–9:30pm daily ■ $

A small, cheerful, and inexpensive restaurant that is frequented by visitors for spicy Indonesian staples such as *sayur lodeh*, a vegetable curry cooked with coconut milk.

6 Lucha Loco
MAP K5 ■ 15 Duxton Hill ■ 3158-3677 ■ Open noon–11pm Mon & Tue (until midnight Wed & Thu, until 1am Fri), 5pm–1am Sat ■ $$

This energetic Mexican restaurant has a great garden-bar and terrace.

7 Blue Ginger
MAP K5 ■ 97 Tanjong Pagar Rd ■ 6222-3928 ■ Open noon–3pm & 6:30–10:30pm daily ■ $$

Blue Ginger is the best place to try delectable Peranakan cuisine.

Quirky interior at Potato Head

8 Potato Head
MAP K4 ■ 36 Keong Saik Rd ■ 6327-1939 ■ Open 11am–midnight daily ■ $$

The international menu makes nods to Asia, but really it is all about the burgers and cocktails here.

9 Annalakshmi
MAP K4 ■ #01-04 Central Square, 20 Havelock Rd ■ 6339-9993 ■ Open 11:15am–3pm & 6:15–10pm daily ■ No prices; payment by donation

Enjoy Indian vegetarian buffets at this place operated by the Temple of Fine Arts, a charity for art and music,

10 Spring Court Restaurant
MAP K4 ■ 52–6 Upper Cross St ■ 6449-5030 ■ Open 11am–3pm & 6–10:30pm daily ■ $$$

Singapore's oldest Chinese restaurant occupies a heritage shophouse.

See map on p70 ←

TOP 10 Little India and Kampong Glam

In the mid-19th century, herders settled and raised cattle in the area that is now Little India. This trade blossomed, supported by Indian labor. The government later opened brick kilns and lime pits that also relied on Indian workers; today, there are stores selling wares from India, just as there would have been 100 years ago. Kampong Glam was allocated to the Sultan of Singapore in Raffles' 1822 town plan and attracted other Muslim residents such as Malays, Bugis (from Sulawesi), and Arabs. Bugis immigrants set up ship-building firms, and some Arab companies are still in business today. Arabic culture is evident in the cafés and stores.

Store selling baskets on Arab Street

1 Arab Street
MAP G4, G5, H5

Named for the Arab traders who were among the earliest foreign settlers, Arab Street is the main thoroughfare in Kampong Glam, Singapore's Muslim quarter. The stores here sell batiks, baskets, fabrics, and items from Indonesia and the Middle East.

2 Serangoon Road
MAP F4, H4

This avenue is the heart of Little India, and feels less slick than the rest of Singapore. Family-run stores still operate from old shophouses, and Indians still come here to buy items such as clothing, groceries, and ceremonial treasures. Inside a few of the stores, spice grinders, laundrymen, and gold-smiths continue to work as they have done for decades.

LITTLE INDIA AND KAMPONG GLAM

Little India and Kampong Glam

③ Sri Srinivasa Perumal Temple

MAP G2 ■ 397 Serangoon Rd ■ 6298-5771 ■ Open 8:30am–noon & 6–9pm daily ■ www.sspt.org.sg

The first temple in Singapore to be built for the worship of Vishnu, Sri Srinivasa Perumal Temple has an impressive *gopuram* (main gate) with more than five tiers of figurines, including representations of Vishnu's various incarnations as well as his steed, the half-man, half-eagle Garuda. Part of the Hindu trinity, Vishnu is associated with protection, as Brahma is with creation, and Shiva with destruction. This is also the start for Thaipusam *(see p66)* and Thimithi *(see p67)*.

Sri Srinivasa Perumal Temple

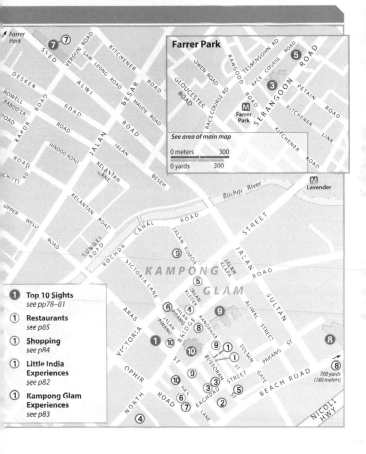

① **Top 10 Sights**
see pp78–81

① **Restaurants**
see p85

① **Shopping**
see p84

① **Little India Experiences**
see p82

① **Kampong Glam Experiences**
see p83

Abdul Gafoor Mosque facade

(4) Abdul Gafoor Mosque

MAP F4, G4 ■ 41 Dunlop St
■ 6295-4209 ■ Open 8am–8pm
(except prayer times) daily; closed
noon–2:30pm Fri

This mosque is a mix of Islamic and European architecture, with stately columns supporting Moorish arches. A sun motif above the main entrance contains names of the 25 prophets of Islam in delicate calligraphy within its rays.

(5) Malay Heritage Centre

MAP H4 ■ 85 Sultan Gate
■ 6391-0450 ■ Compound:
open 8am–9pm daily;
museum: open 10am–6pm
Tue–Sun ■ Adm (museum)
■ www.malayheritage.
gov.sg

This building was originally Istana Kampong Glam, the official residence of the nobility of the Johor sultanate. After several years of restoration, it was converted into the Malay Heritage Centre in 2005.

ISTANA KAMPONG GLAM

In 1824, Sultan Hussein Shah signed away his sovereign rights to the East India Company in return for a plot of land. After his death, his son Sultan Ali built Istana Kampong Glam on the land. In 1905, it became state property. The sultan's descendants were allowed to live in the palace until the 1990s. By 1999, plans were announced to turn the building into the Malay Heritage Centre.

The five galleries follow the layout of a traditional Malay house, showcasing the rich arts and cultural traditions of the Malay community.

(6) Sri Veeramakaliamman Temple

Since its humble beginnings in the mid-19th century, this temple (see pp20–21) has been associated with the laboring classes, as it was built mainly for and by local workers. It was constructed for the worship of Kali, a divine mother figure who provides comfort to worshippers far from home. As with all Hindu temples in Singapore, the colorful figures on the roof were created by skilled craftsmen brought in from southern India especially for the job.

Sri Veeramakaliamman Temple

(7) Mustafa Centre

MAP G3 ■ 145 Syed Alwi Rd ■ 6295-5855 ■ Open 24 hours ■ www.mustafa.com.sg

This enormous department store snakes through two city blocks, offering 24-hour shopping for a huge range of Indian products. There is everything from ordinary, well-discounted store goods to a stunning collection of intricate treasures in the gold department. The store also has a large collection of saris, traditional dress, jewelry, and textiles.

(8) Hajjah Fatimah Mosque

MAP H5 ■ 4001 Beach Rd
■ 6297-2774 ■ Open 10am–9pm daily

A local businesswoman, Hajjah Fatimah, lived at this site in a house that was burgled twice before being set on fire. In gratitude for her escape, she decided to build a mosque here. Built around 1846, the edifice is a mix of European, Chinese, and Malay architecture. Most interesting is the tilting minaret – Singapore's take on Italy's Leaning Tower of Pisa.

9 Sakya Muni Buddha Gaya Temple

MAP G2 ■ 366 Race Course Rd
■ 6294-0714 ■ Open 8am–4:30pm daily

This small Buddhist temple is also known as the Temple of a Thousand Lights, thanks to the 989 lights that surround the main Buddha image, and are turned on for special ceremonies. Around the base of the main altar, painted murals depict episodes from the life of the Buddha. Behind the altar, a small doorway leads to an inner chamber with an image of the reclining Buddha. The temple has many Thai aesthetic influences handed down from its founder, who was a Thai monk.

10 Sultan Mosque

The most important mosque in Singapore, Sultan Mosque (see pp18–19) was built using contributions from the Muslim community. Even glass bottles donated by the poor were used for the band at the base of the onion dome. The mosque's governing body is made up of two members from each ethnic group of the local Muslim community – Malays, Javanese, Bugis, Arabs, Tamils, and North Indians.

Onion dome of the Sultan Mosque

EXPLORING LITTLE INDIA AND KAMPONG GLAM

▶ MORNING

From Little India MRT station, enter the adjacent **Tekka Market** (see p84) which has lively hawker stalls and a wet market at ground level, with clothing stalls above. Then follow the main Serangoon Road north to **Sri Veeramakaliamman Temple** to witness vibrant Hindu traditions. Slightly further along is **Mustafa Centre**, a 24-hour megastore that sells quite possibly everything in its vast and bewildering interior. Farther up Serangoon Road is the large **Sri Srinivasa Perumal Temple** (see p79). Next, take Perumal Road to Race Course Road and turn right to **Sakya Muni Buddha Gaya Temple**. Then head through the backstreets southeast of Serangoon Road, to wander past colorful shophouses and pop into pretty **Abdul Gafoor Mosque**.

AFTERNOON

From Little India, it is a 10-minute walk to **Kampong Glam** and lunch in one of the buzzing resto-bars on Haji Lane (see p83). They all appeal, but a good choice is **Blu Jaz Café** (see p83) for local and international comfort food. Afterwards, check out the independent boutiques along the lane and regional textiles on the adjacent Arab Street. Make a visit to the **Sultan Mosque**, at the heart of this Muslim neighborhood. From there, browse souvenirs along Bussorah Street (see p83) before heading a couple of blocks north to the **Malay Heritage Centre**.

See map on pp78–9 ←

Little India Experiences

Flower garlands for sale on Campbell Lane

1 Flower Garlands
MAP F4 ■ Campbell Lane & Buffalo Rd

Garlands of fresh flowers are sewn together by hand and sold on street corners in this area.

2 Amrita Ayurvedic
MAP F4 ■ 11 Upper Dickson Rd ■ 6299-0642 ■ Open 9am–9pm Wed–Mon

Traditional Indian medicine has been practiced for more than 5,000 years. Amrita uses natural, plant-based formulations for its treatments and also offers yoga classes.

3 Sajeev Studio
MAP F4 ■ 23 Kerbau Rd ■ 6296-6537 ■ Open 11am–8pm daily

This photographer dresses men and women in traditional Indian clothing, jewelry, and make-up for keepsake portraits.

4 Our Lady of Lourdes
MAP G4 ■ 50 Ophir Rd ■ 6294-0624

This historic church bears testimony to the spread of Catholicism in Singapore, especially the growth of the Tamil Catholic community, over the years.

5 Brahma Kumaris
MAP G3 ■ Level 3, Chern Seng Building, 7 Hindoo Rd ■ www.brahma kumaris.org.sg

A spiritual center that offers free yoga and meditation classes.

6 ANSA Picture Framing and Art Gallery
MAP F4 ■ 29 Kerbau Rd ■ 6295-6605 ■ Open 9:30am–9pm Mon–Sat

Browse through portraits of Hindu deities along with secular works.

7 Street Art
MAP F4, F3 & G3 ■ Kerbau Rd, Serangoon Rd, Baboo Lane & Desker Rd

Colorful murals by local and international artists depict vivid scenes, ranging from traditional Indian dances to a tiffin delivery man.

8 Indian Heritage Centre
MAP F4 ■ 5 Campbell Lane ■ 6291-1601 ■ Open 10am–7pm Tue–Thu (until 8pm Fri & Sat, until 4pm Sun) ■ Adm

Five galleries highlight the history of the local Indian community, and there's a free guided tour every day.

Indian Heritage Centre

9 Selvi's
MAP F4 ■ #01–23, 48 Serangoon Rd, Little India Arcade ■ 6297-5322 ■ Open 9am–8:30pm daily (until 5pm Sun)

Artists apply henna, a natural dye, to your hands, leaving a temporary tattoo.

10 Betel Nuts
MAP F4 ■ Campbell Lane & Buffalo Rd

The areca palm seed is wrapped by street sellers in a leaf, to be chewed.

→ *See map on pp78–9*

Kampong Glam Experiences

1 Wardah Books
MAP H5 ▪ 58 Bussorah St
▪ 6297-1232 ▪ Open 10am–7pm daily
(until 9pm Fri & Sat) ▪ www.wardah
books.com

Find locally published fiction,
books on Malay culture, as well
as titles on Southeast Asia and
the Middle East at this bookstore.

2 Kampong Glam Café
MAP H5 ▪ 17 Bussorah St
▪ Open 8–2am Tue–Sun

Popular with locals and tourists
alike, this roadside open-air restaurant serves Malay and Indian food.

3 Bhai Sarbat
MAP H5 ▪ 21 Baghdad St
▪ Open 6:30–1am daily; closed
1–2pm Fri

This stall sells a thick mixture of
sweetened condensed milk and
tea, poured between two cups to
make it frothy (see p57). A popular
local favorite.

4 Parkview Square
MAP G5 ▪ 600 North Bridge Rd

Designed in 2002 in the Art Deco style,
this office tower hosts Atlas (see p58),
one of Singapore's most lavish bars.

5 Bussorah Street
MAP H5 ▪ Bussorah St

A wide, palm-fringed avenue that
has several shops selling antiques,
curios, and souvenirs, plus Arabic
and Turkish restaurants.

6 Hjh Maimunah Restaurant
MAP G4 ▪ 11 & 15 Jalan Pisang
▪ 6297-4294 ▪ Open 7am–8pm
Mon–Sat

A local institution for spicy Malay
food. Go early and join the fast-
moving queue.

7 Blu Jaz Café
MAP H5 ▪ 11 Bali Lane
▪ 6292-3800 ▪ Open noon–1am
Sun–Thu (until 2am Fri & Sat)

This long-standing venue has a
colorful outdoor area as well as
a diverse food menu.

8 Golden Mile Complex
MAP H5 ▪ 5001 Beach Rd
▪ Open 10am–10pm daily

Singapore's Little Thailand attracts
residents with groceries, traditional
goods, and traditional Thai food.

9 Muslim Cemetery
MAP H4 ▪ Corner of Victoria St
& Jalan Kubor

The gravestones look haphazard, but
square stones indicate men's graves,
and round ones mark those of women.

10 Haji Lane
MAP G5, H5 ▪ 15 min walk
from Bugis MRT

A narrow alley with offbeat stores
that sell locally designed clothing
and imported oddities.

Quaint stores on Haji Lane

Shopping

1 Ratianah
MAP H5 ■ 23 Bussorah St
■ 6392-0323 ■ Open 12:30–8pm Tue–
Thu (until 9pm Fri & Sat), 1–7pm Sun
Peranakan-style fabrics, women's
clothes, and some jewelry are sold
at this Malay-run shop.

2 Sri Ghanesh Textiles
MAP F4 ■ 100 Serangoon
Rd ■ 6298-2029 ■ Open 9:30am–
9:30pm daily
Textile shop with a wide assortment
of high-quality saris from India,
Japan, China, and Indonesia.

3 Rishi Handicrafts
MAP H5 ■ 58 Arab St ■ 6298-
2408 ■ Open 10am–6pm daily
All sorts of baskets, woven hats,
mats, and bags, mostly from
Indonesia and China, are available
at this Baghdad Street landmark.

4 StyleMart
MAP F4 ■ 149–151 Selegie Rd
■ 6338-2073 ■ Open 11am–8pm
Mon–Thu (until 9pm Fri & Sat), noon–
7pm Sun
A boutique specializing in fine,
formal Indian fashions, such as
embroidered and beaded silks and
brocades – perfect for gifts.

5 Little India Arcade
MAP F4 ■ 48 Serangoon Rd
■ Open 9am–10pm daily
A cluster of stores here sells
costume jewelry, tapestries,
Bollywood DVDs, incense, leather
goods, and Indian fashions.

Clothes for sale in Tekka Market

6 Tekka Market
MAP F3 ■ 665 Buffalo Rd
■ Open 6am–10pm daily
This landmark building offers a wet
market, hawker stalls, and stores
stocking inexpensive Indian clothing.

7 Mustafa Centre
Although the 24-hour Mustafa
Centre (see p80) sells everything
under the sun, its best offerings are
Indian imports – silk saris, gold
jewelry, and woven textiles.

8 Jamal Kazura Aromatics
MAP H4 ■ 728 North Bridge
Rd ■ 6293-2350 ■ Open 10am–6pm
Mon–Fri (until 2pm Sat)
Find oil-based fragrances at this
store for those who may wish to
avoid contact with alcohol.

9 Basharahil Brothers
MAP H5 ■ 101 Arab St ■ 6296-
0432 ■ Open 10am–5:30pm Mon–Sat,
11am–5pm Sun
Cotton and silk batik cloth, imported
from Indonesia, is sold here by the
meter or in the form of sarongs,
placemats, tablecloths,
and napkins.

10 Asian Arts & Crafts
MAP F3 ■ 180 Serangoon
Rd ■ 6299-0500 ■ 10am–
10pm daily
The store stocks an
array of religious art and
artifacts – mostly Hindu.

Little India Arcade

Restaurants

1 Jaggi's Northern Indian Cuisine

MAP F3 ▪ 34 Race Course Rd ▪ 6296-6141 ▪ Open 11am–10:30pm daily ▪ $

Enjoy delicious Indian curries, plus meats and freshly baked breads from Jaggi's tandoor oven.

2 Komala Vilas

MAP F4 ▪ 76 Serangoon Rd ▪ 6293-6980 ▪ Open 7am–10:30pm daily ▪ $

One of the quickest lunches around. The specialty, *dosai*, is a hot pancake served with gravy. Dishes are vegetarian and very good value.

3 Muthu's Curry

MAP F3 ▪ 138 Race Course Rd ▪ 6392-1722 ▪ Open 10:30am–10:30pm daily ▪ $$

Muthu's is home to Singapore's favourite fish-head curry. Various southern Indian dishes are served, too.

4 Islamic Restaurant

MAP H4 ▪ 745 North Bridge Rd ▪ 6298-7563 ▪ Open 10am–10pm daily; closed 1–2pm Fri ▪ $

Established in 1921, one of the oldest surviving restaurants in Singapore serves meat and seafood dishes.

5 Symmetry

MAP H4 ▪ 9 Jalan Kubor ▪ 6291-9901 ▪ Open 11am–11pm Tue–Thu (until 9pm Mon, until midnight Fri), 9am–midnight Sat (until 7pm Sun) ▪ $$

A casual café and bar by day, this spot becomes a hipster diner at night, serving French-inspired, meat-heavy cuisine with laid-back Australian hospitality. Plates are designed to be shared.

6 Good Luck

MAP H5 ▪ 9 Haji Lane ▪ 6391-9942 ▪ Open noon–late Wed–Mon (from 4pm Tue) ▪ $$

Enjoy burgers and handmade noodles accompanied by craft beers.

7 The Banana Leaf Apolo

MAP F3 ▪ 54 Race Course Rd ▪ 6293-8682 ▪ Open 10:30am–10:30pm daily ▪ $

Named for the leaf on which south Indian cuisine is served, this spot also offers north Indian dishes.

Fish curry, The Banana Leaf Apolo

8 Gokul Vegetarian Restaurant

MAP F4 ▪ 19 Upper Dickson Rd ▪ 6396-7769 ▪ Open 10:30am–10pm daily ▪ $

Gokul offers vegetarian versions of Singapore's most famous dishes.

9 Rumah Makan Minang

MAP H4, H5 ▪ 18 & 18A Kandahar St ▪ 6977-7064 ▪ Open 8:30am–8pm daily ▪ $

This restaurant serves up a delicious beef and chicken *rendang* (curry), among other Indonesian dishes.

10 Zam Zam

MAP G5 ▪ 697–699 North Bridge Rd ▪ 6298-6320 ▪ Open 7am–11pm daily ▪ $

Zam Zam is famed for *murtabak*, an Indian bread filled with onion, meat, and egg, and dipped in curry.

See map on pp78–9 ➡

TOP 10 Civic District

National Museum of Singapore

Before the arrival of Sir Thomas Stamford Raffles, Singapore was a small fishing village surrounded by jungle. In time, the jungle gave way to building programs to house the Malay, and eventually colonial, government. A grand governor's residence, complete with its own botanical gardens, was built on top of the hill overlooking the Civic District. In the 1800s, development increased and the district expanded rapidly; many of the existing buildings date from this era. The oldest part of Singapore is Fort Canning, a hilltop park. Here visitors will find a well-tended grave, believed to be that of Iskandar Shah, who ruled Singapore in the 14th century, but was driven out by the Javanese or Siamese and went on to found Melaka in Malaysia.

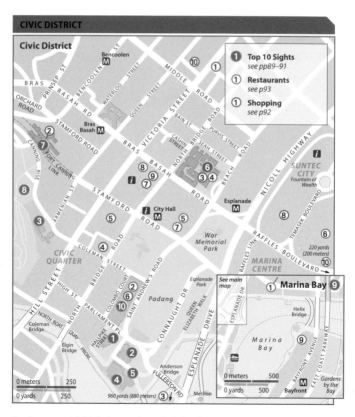

CIVIC DISTRICT

1 Top 10 Sights
see pp89–91

1 Restaurants
see p93

1 Shopping
see p92

Previous pages A brightly decorated street in Little India

The Arts House, Old Parliament House

1 Old Parliament House

Before Raffles' Town Plan was fully implemented *(see p90)*, construction began on Singapore's first modern structure – a mansion for Scottish merchant John Maxwell, built in 1826 and later sold to the government. In 1999, the government moved to the new granite Parliament House next door, and the old building *(see p42)* has been converted into The Arts House.

2 Victoria Theatre and Concert Hall

MAP M3 ■ 11 Empress Place ■ 6602-4200 ■ www.vtvch.com

The Town Hall, completed in 1862, was the first structure purpose-built for the colonial government. The government soon outgrew the premises, and in 1909, the building was converted into a theater. The adjacent concert hall, now home to the Singapore Symphony Orchestra (SSO), was finished in 1905. Both venues were then dedicated to Queen Victoria.

Victoria Theatre and Concert Hall

3 Children's Museum Singapore

MAP L2 ■ 23B Coleman St ■ 6337-3888 ■ Open times vary, check website ■ Adm ■ www.nhb.gov.sg/childrensmuseum

Singapore's first dedicated children's museum encourages kids to explore the country's heritage and diverse culture through its immersive exhibitions, interactive displays, and multi-sensory activities.

4 The Empress Place Building/Asian Civilisations Museum

Since Maxwell's House was too small for the growing colonial administration, a new government office was built. The oldest part was erected in 1864, with three extensions being added before it was reopened in 1905 as the Empress Place Building. It continued to be used for offices until the 1980s. Among these was the Registry of Births and Deaths – it was said that every Singaporean passed through its doors. In 2003, the building became the Asian Civilisations Museum *(see p14)*.

5 Statue of Raffles

MAP M3 ■ 9 Empress Place

This bronze statue of Sir Stamford Raffles was erected at the Padang in 1887, and it was moved to its current location outside the Victoria Theatre and Concert Hall in 1919, to mark Singapore's first centennial. A replica is perched at the spot along the Singapore River where it is believed that Raffles first set foot on the island in 1819.

The beautiful Raffles Hotel building

6 Raffles Hotel

The Civic District has been the location of numerous hotels for European visitors, but only one stands today. Raffles Hotel *(see pp30–31)* was built from an existing bungalow in 1887, and, after extensions and renovations, has grown into an iconic landmark. Its graceful courtyards and cozy bars and restaurants retain a serene atmosphere amid the bustle of the surrounding business district.

7 National Museum of Singapore

The National Museum *(see pp12–13)* has over 198,056 sq ft (18,400 sq m) of exhibit space, with galleries dedicated to presenting Singapore's history and heritage through entertaining multimedia displays. This is a highly recommended introduction to Singapore.

8 Fort Canning Park

MAP K1–2, L1–2 ▪ Canning Rise ▪ Open 24 hours daily ▪ www. nparks.gov.sg

Raffles built his home at this site, but it was replaced by Fort Canning in 1860. The military stronghold atop the park's hill was impressive, but it proved useless protection, as its cannons could not reach as far as the harbor. The fort was demolished in 1929, but a Gothic gate remains. The lawns now host concerts, and the underground bunkers,

Cupolas at Fort Canning Park

known as the Battlebox, function as an interesting World War II exhibit *(see pp44–5)*.

9 Marina Bay

Created over decades by reclaiming land, Marina Bay *(see pp26–7)* effectively extends the Civic District, the financial district, and the Kampong Glam area southward and eastward. The Singapore River now flows into the "bay" – really a freshwater reservoir – with the sea kept out by the Marina Barrage. Surrounding the bay are some top-dollar attractions, notably the Marina Bay Sands hotel and casino, Esplanade, and Gardens by the Bay.

National Gallery Singapore

10 City Hall and the Supreme Court

MAP M2 ■ St. Andrew's Rd

Completed in 1929, City Hall was the site of many historical events. In 1945, the Japanese surrendered here; in 1959, Prime Minister Lee Kuan Yew proclaimed Singapore's self-rule on the steps; and in 1966, it was the site of Singapore's first National Day celebrations. The Supreme Court was built in 1932, and, although both buildings are massive, the government outgrew them. The judiciary now operates from the new Supreme Court building behind the original, while the City Hall offices now occupy other modern buildings. The old buildings now house the National Gallery *(see p40)*.

A WALK AROUND THE CIVIC DISTRICT

MORNING

Begin at the **National Museum** *(see pp12–13)*, where you can spend a couple of hours exploring the history of Singapore. Exit through the rear to walk through **Fort Canning Park** to soak up its heritage and great views. Walk down from the park onto Hill Street, and turn left to admire the 1835 **Armenian Church** *(see p38)*, Singapore's oldest church. Behind the church stands the **Peranakan Museum** *(see p40)*, which illuminates the culture of the Straits Chinese. Next, walk one block up Victoria Street to beautiful **CHIJMES** *(see p43)*, a 19th-century missionary school, which is now a dining and shopping complex.

AFTERNOON

Next to CHIJMES on Bras Basah Road is **Raffles City Shopping Centre**, which has a good mix of luxury and mainstream labels. After a shopping fix, cross Bras Basah to tour the famous **Raffles Hotel** and maybe have a Singapore Sling in the Long Bar. Exit from Raffles' main entrance on Beach Road, turn right and continue on to **St. Andrew's Cathedral** *(see p43)*. After exploring the church's nostalgic interior, follow the road south with the historic **Padang** *(see p45)* to your left and the **National Gallery Singapore** *(see p40)* to your right. Spend the rest of the afternoon at the gallery or, depending on your interests, head past the **Victoria Theatre** *(see p89)* to explore the **Asian Civilisations Museum** *(see p89)*.

See map on p88 ←

Shopping

1 Bugis Street Market
MAP G5 ■ Bugis St ■ Open 2–11pm daily (some stalls open 10am)

This market is packed with stalls selling all kinds of souvenirs.

2 Supermama
MAP L1 ■ National Museum, 93 Stamford Rd ■ 9615-7473 ■ Open 10am–7pm daily

The National Museum's gift shop stocks locally designed souvenirs, clothes, and homewares with a Singaporean touch, featuring nostalgic references or glimpses of local humor.

3 Raffles Boutique
Head here to find every kind of gift, from T-shirts to bone china sets, bearing the Raffles Hotel (see p30) emblem. There is also a gallery and a small café on the premises.

4 Cathay Photo
MAP L2 ■ Peninsula Plaza, 111 North Bridge Rd ■ 6337-4274 ■ Open 10am–7pm Mon–Sat

This camera store offers quality stock at decent prices.

5 Funan
MAP L2 ■ 107 North Bridge Rd ■ 6970-1668

This mall complex (see p62) is home to numerous global brands.

6 The Gallery Store
MAP M2 ■ National Gallery Singapore, 1 St Andrew's Rd ■ 8869-6970 ■ Open 10am–7pm daily

The gift shop at the National Gallery has stylish souvenirs, including clothes, accessories, and homewares, plus a good selection of art books for adults and children.

7 CYC The Custom Shop
MAP M2 ■ #01–12/13/14 Capitol Piazza, 13 Stamford Rd ■ 6336-3556 ■ Open 11am–8pm daily

The attention to detail makes CYC one of the city's finest shirt makers.

8 Royal Selangor
MAP M1 ■ #01–370 Suntec City Mall, 3 Temasek Boulevard ■ 6822-1559 ■ Open 10am–10pm daily

Established in 1885, this shop makes tankards, home accessories, and other pewter products.

9 Arch
MAP M2 ■ #B1-13 Capitol Piazza, 13 Stamford Rd ■ 6384-6608 ■ Open 11:30am–8:30pm daily

This place sells attractive souvenirs, such as images of iconic Singapore buildings and shophouses intricately cut into wooden veneers.

10 Bugis Junction and Bugis+
MAP G5 ■ 200–1 Victoria St ■ Open 10am–10pm daily

These two malls linked by a bridge are hot for high-street brands. Both have a good selection of food and beverage outlets, too.

Bugis Junction and Bugis

Restaurants

PRICE CATEGORIES
For a three-course meal for one with a non-alchoholic drink (or equivalent meal), taxes, and extra charges.

$ under S$30 $$ S$30–70 $$$ over S$70

1 Morton's The Steakhouse
MAP N2 ■ Mandarin Oriental Hotel, 5 Raffles Ave ■ 6339-3740 ■ Open 5:30–11pm Mon–Sat, noon–3pm & 5:30–9pm Sun ■ Reservations advisable ■ $$$

A classic steakhouse (see p58) with one main, and three private dining spaces.

2 National Kitchen by Violet Oon
MAP M2 ■ #02-01 National Gallery, 1 St Andrew's Rd ■ 9834-9935 ■ Open noon–5pm & 6–10:30pm daily ■ www.violetoon.com ■ $$

The dishes here (see p59) include coronation chicken in wantan leaf cup, and an excellent beef rendang.

3 Majestic Restaurant
MAP M5 ■ #04-01 Marina One, 5 Straits View ■ 6250 1988 ■ Open 11:30am–3pm & 5:45–10pm daily ■ www.restaurant majestic.com ■ $$$

Enjoy excellent Cantonese fare at this elegant restaurant (see p58) situated in the heart of Marina Bay.

4 Tiffin Room
MAP M1 ■ 1 Beach Rd ■ 6412-1816 ■ Open noon–2pm & 6:30–10pm daily ■ $$$

Named for the Indian light midday meal, this long-time fixture (see p30) at the Raffles Hotel offers finely spiced North Indian food.

5 Mikuni
MAP M1–M2 ■ Level 3, Fairmont Singapore, 80 Bras Basah Rd ■ 6431-6156 ■ Open noon–10:30pm Mon–Sat ■ www.fairmont.com ■ $$$

Excellent Japanese fare is on offer at this fine dining restaurant (see p59).

6 Rang Mahal
MAP N2 ■ Level 3, Pan Pacific Hotel, 7 Raffles Boulevard ■ 6333-1788 ■ Open times vary, check website ■ www.rangmahal.com.sg ■ $$$

This well-known restaurant (see p59) offers tasty fare from around India.

7 Prego
MAP M1 ■ Fairmont Hotel, 80 Bras Basah Rd ■ 6431-6156 ■ Open 7am–10:30pm daily ■ $$

Enjoy a range of excellent thin-crust pizzas at this Italian restaurant.

8 Lei Garden
MAP M1 ■ #01–24 CHIJMES, 30 Victoria St ■ 6339-3822 ■ Open 11:30am–3:30pm & 6–11pm daily ■ $$

Exquisite Cantonese fine-dining experience within the historic CHIJMES complex (see p43).

Dining space at CUT

9 CUT
MAP P4 ■ #B1-71 The Shoppes at Marina Bay Sands ■ 6688-8517 ■ Open 5pm–midnight daily ■ www.marinabaysands.com ■ $$$

Find great food and excellent service (see p59) at this acclaimed restaurant.

10 Summer Pavilion
MAP N2 ■ Ritz-Carlton Millenia, 7 Raffles Ave ■ 6434-5286 ■ Open 11:30am–2:30pm & 6:30–10:30pm daily ■ www.ritzcarlton.com ■ $$$

A Michelin-starred restaurant (see p59) with exquisite food and specialty teas.

See map on p88

TOP 10 Orchard Road

Orchard Road gets its name from the plantations that were developed here in the 1830s to grow fruit, nutmeg, pepper, and other spices. By the mid-1800s, the plantations had been wiped out by disease and the area began to be developed as a residential suburb. From the late 1800s, many businesses were established to serve the local population of Chinese, Malays, Indians, Jews, and Europeans. In the 1950s, Orchard Road evolved as a retail district. Today, it is famous for its upmarket shops, leisure facilities, and hotels.

The Istana

① The Istana and Sri Temasek

MAP D3, D4 ■ Adm ■ www.istana.gov.sg

The Istana (see p43), which means "palace", was considered expensive for a governor's residence, but, upon the building's completion in 1869, its design won critics over. Situated at the top of a hill, it is surrounded by tropical gardens.

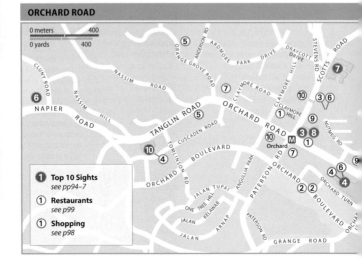

ORCHARD ROAD

- ① **Top 10 Sights** see pp94–7
- ① **Restaurants** see p99
- ① **Shopping** see p98

Colorful houses on Emerald Hill Road

2 Emerald Hill Road
MAP C4–5

Away from Orchard Road, Emerald Hill Road is surprisingly tranquil. A lane of millionaires' homes (some of them now feature stylish bars), the Hill's Peranakan-style row houses have been well restored. There are several house styles, from plain, boxy 19th-century buildings to the pre-war Chinese Baroque-style terrace houses, and even ornate Art Deco variations of the 1950s shophouse.

3 Tangs
MAP B4 ■ 310 Orchard Rd ■ 6737-5500 ■ Open 10:30am–9:30pm Mon–Sat, 11am–8:30pm Sun ■ www.tangs.com

This homegrown department store sprouted from the dreams of a door-to-door salesman who arrived from China in 1923. Called the "Tin Trunk Man," C. K. Tang carried goods in a tin trunk that became his trademark. Tang bought this prime piece of property in 1958. His family still owns the department store and the plot of land on which it sits, located at a busy crossroad. Tangs has two stores in Singapore: Orchard Road and VivoCity (see p62).

4 Ngee Ann City
MAP B4, B5, C4, C5 ■ 391A Orchard Rd ■ Open 10am–10pm daily ■ www.ngeeanncity.com.sg

Owned by the Ngee Ann Kongsi, a clan association, this shopping mall was the largest retail space in the country and home to the biggest department store when it opened in 1993. It continues to make a majestic statement along Orchard Road today. Its largest tenant is Takashimaya, a retail giant in Japan. The mall houses more than 30 restaurants, while book lovers can browse the selection at the expansive Kinokuniya bookstore.

Entrance to Ngee Ann City mall

Street performer on Orchard Road

5 Street Performances
MAP A4–C4, C5–E5
■ Orchard Rd

Singapore liberalized public performance regulations in 2000, paving the way for street musicians, comedians, and magicians. Various international busker festivals invite some of the world's best street performers to work the crowds. The sidewalks on Orchard Road have been widened to accommodate special performance areas for buskers. The tourism board (see p112) provides information about planned busker events.

6 Singapore Botanic Gardens

These lovely gardens (see pp24–5) show visitors the area's agricultural origins, and remind residents that the city was once covered in lush tropical forest. The gardens are a favorite spot for joggers in the mornings, for photographers in the late afternoons, and, on the weekends, for families as well. There are also music performances, and movie screenings by the lakes.

Orchid, Singapore Botanic Gardens

7 Goodwood Park Hotel
MAP B3 ■ 22 Scotts Rd ■ 6737-7411 ■ www. goodwoodpark hotel.com

Built in 1900, this hotel began as the Teutonia Club, an enclave for expatriate Germans. In 1929, it was converted into Goodwood Park Hotel, for businessmen from Malaya. It has withstood both World Wars, and much of the original beauty – fluted columns, delicate woodwork, decorative plasterwork, and graceful archways – has been faithfully restored. There are several award-winning restaurants, too.

THE STAMFORD CANAL

Orchard Road's malls sit above a huge hidden canal that drains storm water, protecting the entire area from flash floods during frequent monsoon downpours. The Stamford Canal begins at Tanglin Road, runs beneath Wisma Atria and Ngee Ann City, and continues past City Hall and into Marina Bay.

Goodwood Park Hotel

8 Crossroads Café
MAP B4 ■ Singapore Marriott Hotel, 320 Orchard Rd ■ 6831-4605 ■ Open 7am–midnight Sun–Thu (until 2am Fri & Sat) ■ www.singapore marriott.com

One of Singapore's best spots for people-watching, this café sits at the city's busiest intersection between Orchard, Scotts, and Paterson roads. The sidewalks teem with bustling shoppers. Virtually every visitor passes this spot, as do locals who come to Orchard Road for the malls, teenagers who flock here to hang out, and, on weekends, foreign domestic helpers who gather to catch up with friends.

Skateboarding at Skate Park

9 Skate Park and *SCAPE
MAP C5 ■ 2 Orchard Link ■ www.scape.sg

The skate park hums into the night, while the adjacent *SCAPE creative space attracts the city's youth with free gigs, dance events, and festivals. Young locals also congregate at the neighboring Cathay Cineleisure for movie screenings and to browse the stalls at *SCAPE marketplace.

10 Tanglin Mall
MAP A4 ■ Tanglin Rd

Known as an expat enclave, Tanglin Mall is a popular place for expatriates to shop for imported groceries and special goods. The US, UK, and Australian embassies and the British Council are steps away.

A STROLL ALONG ORCHARD ROAD

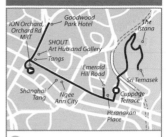

▶ MORNING

Start at Orchard Road MRT station, which will plunge you straight into multilevel **ION Orchard** (see p63) for designer and mainstream shopping. Be sure to visit ION Sky on the 56th floor for 360-degree city views, before crossing Orchard Road to the iconic **Tangs** department store (see p95). From Tangs, swing down Scotts Road to **SHOUT Art Hub and Gallery** (see p98) and the elegant **Goodwood Park Hotel**. Back on Orchard, the next mall stop is **Ngee Ann City** (see p95), where you can browse in the city's largest bookstore, Kinokuniya Singapore, or visit **Shanghai Tang** for contemporary Chinese-inspired design (see p98). Continue down Orchard Road to the junction at Peranakan Place on your left. This nook has good cafés for people-watching.

AFTERNOON

From Peranakan Place, enter **Emerald Hill Road** (see p95) to view enviable private homes converted from Peranakan shophouses (No. 6 retains many original details). Walk back to Orchard Road, where detours into the many malls can occupy the rest of the afternoon. You can refresh yourself with a drink at nearby **Cuppage Terrace**, popular with expats and tourists, or try a local dessert at a food court (there's one in every mall). On selected public holidays, you can visit **the Istana and Sri Temasek** (see p94), located past the intersection with Clemenceau Avenue

See map on pp94–5 ←

Shopping

Asian-inspired clothing and homewares for sale at Shanghai Tang

1 Tangs
This enduring, home-grown department store *(see p95)* offers a broad range of fashion.

2 Takashimaya
MAP B4 ▪ 391 Orchard Rd ▪ 6738-1111 ▪ Open 10am–9:30pm daily
One of Japan's oldest retailers, this huge store stocks apparel, cosmetics, and household items.

3 Paragon
One of the several Orchard Road malls, Paragon *(see p63)* makes a play for high-end custom and is home to Armani, Calvin Klein, and Gucci, among other big names.

4 Kinokuniya Singapore
MAP B4 ▪ #04–20 Ngee Ann City, 391 Orchard Rd ▪ 6737-5021 ▪ Open 10am–9:30pm Sun–Fri (until 10pm Sat)
A quality bookstore with an excellent selection of fiction and non-fiction, plus magazines, including some foreign-language titles.

5 Naga Arts & Antiques
MAP A4 ▪ #01–48 Tanglin Shopping Centre, 19 Tanglin Rd ▪ 6235-7084 ▪ Open 10:30am–5:30pm Mon–Sat
With a wide range of Southeast Asian furniture, Buddha images, and textiles, Naga is a paradise for bargain-hunters.

6 Shanghai Tang
MAP B4 ▪ #03–06 Ngee Ann City ▪ 6737-3537 ▪ Open 10am–9:30pm daily
A luxury brand featuring clothing and homeware inspired by China's fashion heritage, with a modern twist.

7 Charles & Keith
MAP C5 ▪ #02–46, 313 Somerset Rd ▪ 6509-5040 ▪ Open 11am–10pm daily
Popular Singapore fashion and accessories brand specializing in women's shoes, bags, and belts.

8 Design Orchard
MAP C5 ▪ 250 Orchard Rd ▪ 6513-1743 ▪ Open 10:30am–9:30pm Sun–Fri (until 10:30pm Sat)
A shared workspace and retail outlet for Singapore's designers, selling clothes, homeware, and souvenirs.

9 SHOUT Art Hub and Gallery
MAP B4 ▪ Scotts Sq, 6 Scotts Rd ▪ 8909-8024 ▪ Open 11am–7pm daily
Find contemporary street and pop art by local and international artists here.

10 T Galleria by DFS
MAP B4 ▪ 25 Scotts Rd ▪ 6229-8100 ▪ Open 11am–8pm Sun–Thu (until 9pm Fri & Sat)
The world's largest duty-free luxury-goods retailer delivers purchases to the airport to pick up on departure.

Restaurants

① Les Amis
MAP B4 ▪ #01–16 Shaw Centre, 1 Scotts Rd ▪ 6733-2225 ▪ Open noon–2:30pm & 7–10pm daily ▪ $$$

The contemporary French menu here has won countless awards.

② Crystal Jade Palace
MAP B4 ▪ #04–19 Takashimaya Shopping Centre, 391 Orchard Rd ▪ 6735-2388 ▪ Open 11:30am–10:30pm Mon–Fri (from 11am Sat, 10am Sun) ▪ $$

The flagship restaurant of the Crystal Jade chain serves Cantonese dishes.

③ mezza9
MAP B4 ▪ Grand Hyatt, 10 Scotts Rd ▪ 6732-1234 ▪ Open noon–2:30pm Mon–Sat & 6–10pm daily (Sunday brunch until 3pm) ▪ $$$

Find Asian and Western dishes at this restaurant, patisserie, and martini bar.

④ Patara Fine Thai
#03–14 Tanglin Mall ▪ 6737-0818 ▪ Open noon–3pm & 6–10:30pm daily ▪ $$

Thai food is complemented by interesting Western flavors.

Buffet spread at The Line

⑤ The Line
MAP A3 ▪ Shangri-La Hotel, 22 Orange Grove Rd ▪ 6213-4398 ▪ Open 12:30–2:30pm & 6–9:30pm Thu–Sun (à la carte menu available 12:30–9:30pm daily) ▪ $$$

A vast buffet of 16 food stations serves tandoori, sushi, salads, and pasta.

⑥ StraitsKitchen
MAP B4 ▪ Grand Hyatt, 10 Scotts Rd ▪ 6732-1234 ▪ Open 7:30am–9:30pm daily ▪ $$

Enjoy a gastronomic experience at this excellent buffet featuring Chinese, Indian, Malay, and Peranakan dishes.

⑦ Hua Ting Restaurant
MAP A3, A4 ▪ Orchard Hotel, 442 Orchard Rd ▪ 6739-6666 ▪ Open 11:30am–2:30pm & 6–10pm daily (from 11am Sat & Sun) ▪ $$

This is the place to visit for a wide range of delicious dim sum and fine traditional Cantonese dishes.

⑧ Tandoor Indian Restaurant
MAP D5 ▪ Holiday Inn Orchard City Centre, 11 Cavenagh Rd ▪ 6733-8333 ▪ Open noon–2:30pm & 7–10:30pm daily ▪ $$

An award-winning place serving terrific north Indian food.

⑨ Tambuah Mas
MAP A4 ▪ #04–10 Tanglin Shopping Centre, 19 Tanglin Rd ▪ 6733-3333 ▪ Open 11am–10pm daily ▪ $$

Serving proper Indonesian home-style cooking for nearly 30 years, Tambuah Mas also has a branch in Paragon (see p63). The tahu telur (crisp-fried beancurd) is a must-try.

⑩ LingZhi
MAP B4 ▪ #05-01 Liat Towers, 541 Orchard Rd ▪ 6734-3788 ▪ Open 11am–3pm & 6–10pm daily ▪ $$

Diners can enjoy sophisticated vegetarian Chinese food that makes inventive use of unusual ingredients and seasonings.

See map on pp94–5

🔟 Farther Afield

Singapore is only 281 sq miles (728 sq km) in size with 120 miles (193 km) of shoreline. The urban center sits at the southernmost tip of the island. At the city's outskirts, pre-war neighborhoods consist of low-rise streets with stores where traditional trades are still practiced. Beyond these, new towns – clusters of high-rise apartment buildings – are supported by schools, businesses, and other facilities. Most new towns enjoy fast links with the city via Mass Rapid Transit trains, operating on several lines.

Henderson Waves bridge

1 The Southern Ridges
MAP S3 ■ Henderson Rd
■ Open 24 hours daily ■ www.nparks.gov.sg

Four parks along the coast – Mount Faber Park, Telok Blangah Hill Park, Kent Ridge Park, and West Coast Park – are connected by a series of bridges, notably the dramatic Henderson Waves. They offer some good views of Sentosa, Keppel Harbour, and the western city center.

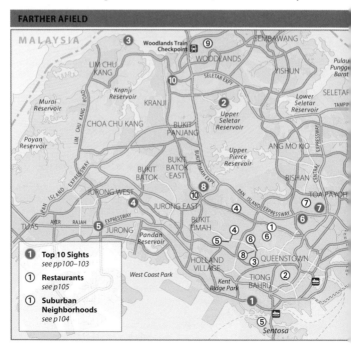

FARTHER AFIELD

1 **Top 10 Sights**
see pp100–103

1 **Restaurants**
see p105

1 **Suburban Neighborhoods**
see p104

Singapore Zoo and Night Safari

② Singapore Zoo, Night Safari, and River Wonders

Three zoos are nestled side by side in northern Singapore, about an hour's journey from the city center. The oldest, Singapore Zoo, has guided tours of its spacious rainforest environment. The Night Safari is a novel way to see nocturnal animals at their most active. River Wonders celebrates the wildlife of the world's great rivers.

③ Sungei Buloh Wetland Reserve

MAP R1 ■ 301 Neo Tiew Crescent ■ 6794-1401 ■ Open 7am–7pm daily ■ www.nparks.gov.sg

A series of paths and walkways leads visitors through mangrove swamps, mudflats, and pools, past an abundance of wildlife. The visitors' center shows a film featuring information on the park's history.

④ Chinese and Japanese Gardens

MAP R2 ■ 1 Chinese Garden Rd ■ Open 5:30am–11pm daily (Chinese Garden), 5:30am–7pm daily (Japanese Garden)

Designed to resemble an imperial garden, the arched bridges, moon gates, and twin pagodas of the Chinese Garden blend with bamboo groves, trees, and flowering shrubs. A Suzhou-style courtyard provides a serene backdrop for the garden's collection of bonsai. The adjoining Japanese Garden has a minimalist Zen feel, with pebble paths and landscaping to evoke contemplation.

⑤ Jurong Bird Park

MAP R2 ■ 2 Jurong Hill ■ 6265-0022 ■ Open 8:30am–6pm daily ■ Adm ■ www.birdpark.com.sg

Visitors can easily spend half a day exploring the world's largest walk-in aviary and tons of other attractions at the bird park, including the huge collection of bird species that are native to Southeast Asia. Plans are underway to move the bird park to the Mandai nature precinct, close to the zoo and other wildlife parks, where it will be renamed as Bird Paradise.

Jurong Bird Park

Sun Yat Sen Nanyang Memorial Hall, with a statue of Sun Yat Sen in front

6 Sun Yat Sen Nanyang Memorial Hall

MAP T2 ▪ 12 Tai Gin Rd ▪ 6256-7377 ▪ Open 10am–5pm Tue–Sun ▪ Adm ▪ www.sysnmh.org.sg

This grand 19th-century bungalow was a private residence before it was donated by a local businessman to Chinese revolutionary Dr. Sun Yat Sen for use as the headquarters of his operations in Southeast Asia. In 1911, after Dr. Sun's Kuomintang Party deposed China's Qing dynasty, it was entrusted to the local Chinese Chamber of Commerce. The bungalow is now a heritage property under the National Heritage Board. The memorial hall traces Dr. Sun's revolutionary activities and highlights the impact of the 1911 Chinese Revolution on Singapore. It also documents the city's contribution to the Revolution.

7 Lian Shan Shuang Lin Monastery

MAP T2 ▪ 184 Jalan Toa Payoh ▪ 6259-6924 ▪ Open 6:30am–5pm daily

Singapore's oldest Buddhist monastery, whose name means "Twin Grove of the Lotus Mountain Temple," claims a 124-year history. It has three main halls – the Hall of Celestial Kings, the Mahavira Hall, and the Dharma Hall, each one built in the typical architectural style of China's southern Fujian province. The

Detail, Lian Shan Shuang Lin Monastery

compound contains a soaring seven-story granite pagoda.

8 Bukit Timah Nature Reserve

MAP S2 ▪ 177 Hindhede Drive ▪ Open 7am–7pm daily ▪ www.nparks.gov.sg

A rare chance to experience primary rainforest within a city, this large nature reserve has four hiking trails, taking up to two hours to complete. The park is home to a variety of birds, insects, and small mammals.

It adheres to conservation acts to protect its biodiversity and prohibits activities that may disturb the flora and fauna, such as feeding the long-tailed macaques. The visitors' center provides useful information to help guests navigate their way, as well as restrooms, and a first-aid station.

9 Pulau Ubin
MAP V1 ■ Ferries run dawn to dusk daily ■ www.nparks.gov.sg

This sleepy rural island lies off Singapore's northeast coast, reached by a ferry ride from Changi Point. Rental bikes are available from the village, where there are also some restaurants. The peaceful tracks are best explored by bike, and there is also a mountain biking trail. Chek Jawa Wetlands has a boardwalk, from which you can spot marine life at low tide.

Jejawi Observation Tower, Pulau Ubin

10 Kranji War Memorial and Cemetery
MAP R1 ■ 9 Woodlands Rd ■ Open 7am–6pm daily

This serene cemetery, overlooking the Strait of Johor, is lined by 4,000 tombstones that mark the graves of the Australians, British, Canadians, Indians, and Malays who lost their lives during World War II. A memorial is dedicated to soldiers whose remains were never recovered.

A DAY TRIP FROM THE CITY

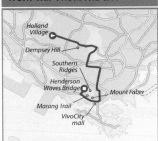

▶ MORNING

Have breakfast in **Holland Village** *(see p104)*. You can choose from its trendy cafés and bakeries, or opt for the Holland Village Market and Food Centre, a two-minute walk from the Holland Village MRT station. Then soak in the laid-back vibe of the neighborhood and explore its many shops. Lim's *(#02-01 Holland Rd Shopping Centre; 6466-3188)* is known for its Peranakan ornaments and crafts by local artisans. Visit the homegrown label Atelier Ong Shunmugan *(43 Jalan Merah Saga, #01-76 Chip Bee Gardens; 6252-2612U)*, offering Asian-inspired womens' wear, or Bynd Artisan *(44 Jalan Merah Saga, #01-54 Chip Bee Gardens; 6475-1680)* for its custom paper and leather goods.

Afterwards, take a short taxi ride or hop on a bus *(nos. 106, 75, or 77)* down Holland Road to **Dempsey Hill** *(see p104)*, where lunch in a leafy setting awaits.

AFTERNOON

Take a taxi to the **Southern Ridges** *(see p100)* for a walk through leafy jungle landscapes. A good starting point for the Ridges is HarbourFront, at the end of the MRT's Circle Line. Pick up some refreshments in **VivoCity mall** *(see p62)* before walking up **Marang Trail** for spectacular views from **Mount Faber**. Continue west to cross the **Henderson Waves Bridge**, which is especially atmospheric as darkness sets in.

See map on pp100–101

Suburban Neighborhoods

1 Geylang
MAP T2

Little visited by tourists, Geylang is an old suburb that can feel like a much less slick version of Chinatown. The nearby Geylang Serai stands out for its distinctly Malay character.

2 Tiong Bahru
MAP S3

Tiong Bahru began to develop before World War II as a new suburb, and has preserved its Art Deco buildings. It is also turning into a hub for creative artists, offering a blend of old and new. The hawker center is a must-see.

3 Katong/Joo Chiat
MAP T2

A melting-pot of Peranakan, Malay, Eurasian, Indian, and Chinese cultures, these two areas promise a treasure trove of places to eat.

Traditional houses in Katong

4 Bukit Timah
MAP S2

This sprawling suburb has several nature trails, including the hike up Singapore's highest hill. Diverse dining can be found on Sixth and Greenwood avenues.

5 Holland Village
MAP S3

Singapore's original expatriate enclave has some interesting Asian art, besides stores selling gifts and home furnishings. With trendy side-walk cafés and bars, too, it appeals to residents of various nationalities who rub shoulders here every day.

6 Dempsey Hill
MAP S2

A cluster of former military barracks set close to the Botanic Gardens, Dempsey Hill offers one-stop shopping for art, antiques, carpets, and home decor. The area's cafés, bars, and restaurants are popular on weekends and evenings.

7 Toa Payoh
MAP T2

A prime example of a New Town, Toa Payoh is centrally located and packed with high-rise apartments, with a busy mall that serves the local community. Many of the stores have been here for decades.

8 Changi Point
MAP V1

This rural seaside village has an open-air hawker center, golf course, a good beach for watersports, and a ferry terminal where you can pick up boats to Palau Ubin.

9 Woodlands
MAP S1

Singapore's last town before reaching Malaysia, Woodlands has a surprisingly large shopping mall, alongside a big American community that has settled here to be close to the Singapore American School.

10 Pasir Ris
MAP U2

A modern New Town, Pasir Ris is located by the sea, with beaches, watersports, waterfront parks, family activities, and alfresco hawker centers and restaurants.

Restaurants

PRICE CATEGORIES
For a three-course meal for one with a non-alcoholic drink (or equivalent meal), taxes, and extra charges.

$ under S$30 $$ S$30–70 $$$ over S$70

1 Atout
MAP S3 ■ 40C Harding Rd ■ 8799-4567 ■ Open noon–10:30pm Mon–Thu (until 11pm Fri & Sat) ■ $$$
Headed by Chef Patrick Heuberger, this French restaurant specializes in charcuterie. There are seafood, meat, and vegetarian options as well.

2 Long Phung Vietnamese
MAP T3 ■ 159 Joo Chiat Rd ■ 6440-6959 ■ Open noon–11pm daily ■ $
A simple, traditional restaurant in lively Joo Chiat that stays crowded late into the night. Pho noodle soup is its specialty, but all dishes are generous and usually super spicy.

3 Samy's Curry Restaurant
MAP S3 ■ 25 Dempsey Rd ■ 6472-2080 ■ Open 11am–3pm & 6–10pm Wed–Mon & public hols ■ $
Visit this Indian restaurant, occupying an open-air hall amid trees, for its chicken masala and fish head curry.

4 Original Sin
MAP S3 ■ #01–62, 43 Jalan Merah Saga, Holland Village ■ 6475-5605 ■ Open 11:30am–2:30pm & 6–10:30pm daily ■ $$
Here you can enjoy Mediterranean vegetarian food enhanced with fresh ingredients and herbs, all complemented by fine wines.

5 TungLok Heen
MAP S3 ■ Lobby Level, Hotel Michael, Resorts World Sentosa ■ 6884-7888 ■ Open 11:30am–3pm & 6–10pm daily ■ www.tunglokheen.com ■ $$$
Known for Chinese cuisine, this *(see p58)* is a gastronomic delight.

6 Grand Shanghai
MAP T3 ■ 390 Havelock Rd ■ 6836-6866 ■ Open 11:30am–2:30pm & 6:30–10:30pm Tue–Sun ■ $$
Shanghainese classics are served in a 1920s ambience. The crispy eels and dim sum are favorites.

Singapore black pepper crab

7 Long Beach Seafood
MAP U3 ■ East Coast Seafood Centre, 1202 East Coast Parkway ■ 6448-3636 ■ Open 11am–11pm daily ■ $$
Famed for its Sri Lankan crabs in black pepper sauce, Long Beach also serves great meat dishes.

8 Candlenut
MAP S3 ■ Block 17A Dempsey Rd ■ 6486-1051 ■ Open noon–3pm & 6–10pm Mon–Sun ■ www.como dempsey.sg ■ $$$
The à la carte and tasting menus *(see p59)* offer Straits-Chinese cuisine.

9 Chilli Padi Nonya Restaurant
MAP T2 ■ 11 Joo Chiat Place ■ 6275-1002 ■ Open 11:30am–2:30pm & 5:30–10pm daily ■ $
This award-winning restaurant offers a selection of Peranakan favorites – unique Straits Chinese cuisine.

10 Al-Azhar
MAP S2 ■ 11 Cheong Chin Nam Rd, Bukit Timah ■ 6466-5052 ■ Open 24 hours daily ■ $
Serving *Mughlai* (Mughal Indian) food, this restaurant is close to the Bukit Timah Nature Reserve.

See map on pp100–101

Streetsmart

Traditional Peranakan shophouse in Chinatown

Getting Around

Arriving by Air

Changi Airport is a main hub through which more than 100 airlines operate in and out of Singapore. There are frequent direct flights to major cities including London, New York, Paris, and Sydney. Several low-cost carriers, such as **Scoot**, **Jetstar**, and **AirAsia**, offer budget flights across the region.

Free English-language tours of the city are available for stopover travelers with a wait of more than 5.5 hours, subject to entry visa regulations. Tour registration is in the transit areas of Terminals 2 and 3. There are multiple tours every day, each lasting 2.5 hours.

From Changi, it is easy to get to the city by the **MRT** subway train, bus, taxi, or the airport shuttle bus, which stops at many downtown hotels. It is about 11 miles (17 km) to downtown, a journey that takes around 1 hour by public transport, or about 25 minutes in a taxi or shuttle bus. There are taxi stands at each of the airport terminals.

Arriving by Train

Rail passengers arrive into Malaysia's Johor Bahru Sentral Railway Station, and change trains to cross the causeway to Woodlands Station in north Singapore. From here, there are frequent MRT trains, buses, and taxis to the city center.

For a luxury experience, the **Belmond** Eastern and Oriental Express travels between Bangkok and Singapore, once or twice per month, from September to December.

Arriving by Bus

From Malaysia, direct international buses terminate at various points in Singapore, depending on which company is operating them. Most arrival points are fairly central, and are connected to onwards public transport.

Non-direct buses go from Johor Bahru in Malaysia to Woodlands or Kranji terminals in northern Singapore, from where buses or the MRT go to the city. Passengers must get off the bus to cross the checkpoint, and board another bus on the Singaporean side. **SBS Transit** and **Causeway Link** have more information.

Arriving by Sea

Ferries serving the Indonesian Riau Islands, notably Batam and Bintan, arrive at the **Singapore Cruise Centre** at HarbourFront and the Tanah Merah Ferry Terminal in eastern Singapore. HarbourFront has its own MRT station, while the Tanah Merah Ferry Terminal is well served by buses.

Public Transport

The **LTA** (Land Transport Authority) runs Singapore's extensive public transport system. Safety and hygiene measures, timetables, ticket information, transport maps, information about taxis, and driving, and more can be viewed on the website.

Travel Passes

Prepaid **EZ-Link** cards are an excellent way of paying for public transport. They are available at many MRT stations or any 7Eleven store, and can be used on the MRT, LRT (overground light railway), buses, and river boats.

One-, two-, or three-day tourist passes are also available from Changi Airport and MRT stations, or at the **Singapore Tourist Pass** website. These allow unlimited travel on the MRT, LRT, and buses.

MRT

The efficient and cheap MRT network operates six lines that run from around 5:40am to midnight. It covers the city center, as well as a majority of attractions in outlying areas. Location maps and clear signage at every station make it very easy to use.

Buses

Singapore has a good network of clean, air-conditioned buses that run throughout the island. Fares vary according to distance and are similar to the price of the MRT. Some find the bus transport map complicated to understand so smartphone transport apps are very useful for planning.

Driving

All of the major car-rental companies operate in Singapore, and the rental process is simple for holders of an international driving permit or an English-language license. However, given the ease of public transport, cheap price of taxis, logistics of parking, and various road tolls, renting a car is not hugely popular.

Taxis

City taxis are relatively inexpensive, although a complex system of peak hour extras and other surcharges can increase fares significantly. Rush hour and rainstorms can make it hard to find a cab. Wait at a taxi stand (compulsory in the city center) or use a smartphone app to book a pick up (additional fees may apply). For three or more people, a taxi is an economical and fast way to get around the city. **Comfort and CityCab** is Singapore's largest taxi company. The **Grab** app is a popular alternative to traditional taxis.

Boats

The 40-minute **Singapore River Cruise** chugs past Robertson Quay, Clarke Quay, and Boat Quay out into Marina Bay. On tourist boats, a commentary is given via a pre-recorded tape. You can also use an EZ-Link card to pay for a "river taxi" ride, without commentary. These boats can be boarded at several stops along the Singapore River between 8am to 10am, and 5pm to 7pm Monday to Friday.

Cycling

Roads in Singapore's city center tend to be busy and few have bike lanes. In general, cycling along the island's wide, fast highways is not recommended. However, many suburban parks and some areas such as Pulau Ubin and the Bukit Timah Nature Reserve are linked by the **PCN** (Park Connector Network) of trails. Bike-rental outfits are limited to the East Coast Parkway, coastal parks such as at Changi Beach, Punggol, and Sentosa. The main provider of dockless bikes for rent is **SG Bike**.

Car-Free Sundays are declared several times a year in certain city center areas to encourage people to see Singapore on foot or by bike.

Walking

Singapore's city center is compact and easy to explore on foot. Plan longer walking routes carefully, because Singapore's heat and humidity can make even a short stroll tiring during the day. Carry water to keep rehydrated, and take advantage of the air conditioning in the city's malls when you want to cool down. Walking at night-time, when the temperature drops, is pleasant and safe, and streets and parks remain well lit.

DIRECTORY

ARRIVING BY AIR

AirAsia
🔲 airasia.com

Changi Airport
🔲 changiairport.com

Jetstar
🔲 jetstarasia.com

MRT
🔲 smrt.com.sg

Scoot
🔲 flyscoot.com

ARRIVING BY TRAIN

Belmond
🔲 belmond.com

ARRIVING BY BUS

Causeway Link
🔲 causewaylink.com.my

SBS Transit
🔲 sbstransit.com.sg

ARRIVING BY SEA

Singapore Cruise Centre
🔲 singaporecruise.com.sg

PUBLIC TRANSPORT

LTA
🔲 lta.gov.sg

TRAVEL PASSES

EZ-Link
🔲 ezlink.com.sg

Singapore Tourist Pass
🔲 thesingapore
touristpass.com.sg

TAXIS

Comfort and Citycab
🔲 cdgtaxi.com.sg

Grab
🔲 grab.com

BOATS

Singapore River Cruise
🔲 rivercruise.com.sg

CYCLING

PCN
🔲 nparks.gov.sg

SG Bike
🔲 sgbike.com.sg

Practical Information

Passports and Visas

Visitors to Singapore require a passport that is valid for at least six months. Most tourists are issued a social visit pass on arrival (free), which is valid for up to 30 or 90 days depending on nationality. US, Australian, UK, and EU tourists can enter without a visa for up to 90 days. Citizens of other countries must apply for a visa in advance (for a fee of S$30), through the **Immigration & Checkpoints Authority** website.

Government Advice

Now more than ever, it is important to consult both your and the Singaporean government's advice before traveling. The **US Department of State**, the **Australian Department of Foreign Affairs and Trade**, the **UK Foreign & Commonwealth Office** and the **Government of Singapore** offer the latest information on security, health and local regulations.

Customs Information

You can find comprehensive information on the laws relating to goods and currency taken in or out Singapore on the **Singapore Customs** website.

Insurance

We recommend taking out a comprehensive insurance policy covering theft, loss of belongings, medical care, cancellations and delays, and reading the small print carefully. The healthcare available in Singapore is very expensive, so it is even more important to have good medical cover.

Health

Singapore's healthcare is known to be one of the best in the world. The most central hospitals are **Gleneagles Hospital**, **Mount Elizabeth Hospital**, **Raffles Hospital**, and **Singapore General Hospital**. They all have 24-hour walk-in accident and emergency departments. Pharmacies provide advice on minor ailments. There are branches of Guardian and Watsons pharmacies in most shopping malls, and some 24-hour pharmacies in the center. Prescriptions from overseas doctors are not accepted.

There are no mandatory inoculations for Singapore, but it is recommended that all travelers have up-to-date hepatitis A & B, diphtheria, tetanus, and typhoid shots. For information regarding COVID-19 vaccination requirements, consult government advice. Singapore has been free of malaria for decades, but dengue still poses a problem. Using mosquito repellent (available at pharmacies) is advisable in the evenings.

Tap water is generally safe to drink except on Pulau Ubin, where it's best to drink bottled water. Food courts have hygiene standards rated by the government, the highest being "A."

Smoking, Alcohol, and Drugs

Smoking is not allowed in most indoor public spaces. However, some premises have designated areas for smoking. Smokers are liable to pay a fine of S$200 if caught smoking in prohibited places, or up to S$1,000 if convicted in court.

The legal drinking age in Singapore is 18 and only those above the age of 18 may purchase alcohol. It is illegal to drink alcohol between 10:30pm and 7am in public places. Those buying alcoholic drinks in restaurants and bars must finish drinking them by 10:30pm. Anybody who violates these rules may face heavy fines. Sale of alcohol at supermarkets and convenience stores is also prohibited during these hours.

Singapore has some of the strictest drug laws in the world. The penalty for possession or consumption of controlled drugs is a maximum of 10 years' imprisonment, or a fine of S$20,000, or both. For a full list of controlled drugs, consult the Government of Singapore website.

ID

It is not a legal requirement to carry ID at all times but having a copy of your passport on you is recommended.

Personal Security

Singapore is an extremely safe city. Laws are strictly enforced, and many minor offences, including smoking in prohibited places, jaywalking, and even chewing gum (except for medicinal purposes), carry a fine. However, petty theft does sometimes occur, so use common sense: keep belongings close and be alert to your surroundings, especially in crowded places. If you have anything stolen, report the crime within 24 hours to the nearest police station and take your passport with you. If you need to make an insurance claim, get a copy of the crime report. Contact your embassy if your passport is stolen, or in the event of a serious crime or accident. For emergency **police** call 999. For medical emergencies call an **ambulance** or in case of **fire** call 995.

Homosexuality is illegal in Singapore and there are no anti-discrimination laws in place. Perceived violation could result in two years in prison though this is very rarely enforced. While many LGBTQ+ people feel relatively safe, they don't necessarily feel accepted in Singapore's largely conservative society. Visitors should be aware that overt displays of affection (regardless of sexual orientation) may attract raised eyebrows. Nethertheless, attitudes among young generations are much more embracing and there are a number of LGBTQ+ bars and clubs with a lively scene in Chinatown, mainly on and around Neil Road. For more information, consult **Oogachaga**, which offers resources and support for the LGBTQ+ community.

Travelers With Specific Requirements

Singapore is one of the most accessible destinations in Asia. Stepless access to buildings and curb ramps are ubiquitous, and the MRT and buses are wheelchair-friendly, and have braille plates and tactile ground surface indicators. Taxis accommodate manual wheelchairs, which must be folded or stored in the boot. Many hotels have accessible rooms with roll-in showers and toilets with grab bars. Those with specific requirements and their caregivers receive free or discounted entry to national museums. The Singapore Tourism Board's website, **Visit Singapore**, has more information.

Time Zone

Singapore is 8 hours ahead of GMT, 12 or 13 hours ahead of New York, and 2 or 3 hours behind Sydney. There is no daylight saving time in Singapore; sunrise and sunset are around 7am and 7pm all year round.

Money

The unit of currency is the Singapore dollar, written S$, which is made up of 100 cents. The Brunei dollar is at par with the Singapore dollar and is legal tender in Singapore. ATMs can be found at banks, shopping malls, and MRT stations. Credit cards such as Visa, American Express, and Mastercard, including contactless payments, are widely accepted in shops, restaurants, and on public transport. The exception are hawker centers and food courts for which you should carry some cash.

Currency can be changed at any hotel or bank, but the best rates are given by the licensed money-changers who operate from booths in shopping centers and commercial hubs. Licensed changers will not charge a commission.

Tipping is generally not customary. Many restaurants add a 10 percent service charge to the bill but a small tip is appreciated if staff have gone out of their way. At higher-end hotels tip porters S$2–S$5 and housekeeping S$2 per day. Round up taxi fares or ask the driver to keep the change.

Electrical Appliances

Singapore's electricity is modeled on the British system of 220–240 volts. Power plugs are of the three-pin type. Hotels usually have adaptors they can loan guests.

Cell Phones and Wi-Fi

Singapore operates on the GSM network, so most cell phones brought overseas will work with a local SIM card inserted. If your phone is network-locked, ask your home carrier for the unlock code to use a different SIM card. There are three local service providers: **M1**, **SingTel**, and **StarHub**. They all offer prepaid SIM cards and data plans, sold at kiosks, phone stores, 7Elevens, and at Changi Airport. Note that with most prepaid deals, incoming calls are charged as well.

Major international hotels provide in-room, high-speed Internet access. There are free Wi-Fi hotspots in the city via the Wireless@SG network, which requires users to register with a foreign or local mobile number. Many shopping malls offer free Wi-Fi.

Postal Services

SingPost provides efficient mail-and-package handling from post offices and kiosks at MRT stations and shopping malls.

Weather

Singapore's temperature remains fairly constant throughout the year, with an average high of 31° C (88° F) and relative humidity of 85 per cent. Rainfall is highest November–January and lowest June–July. Peak travel season is from June to September. Around mid-December is also a busy time.

Opening Hours

Banks are open between 9:30am and 3pm Monday to Friday and until 1pm on Saturday. Shops and malls are generally open from 10am to 10pm, and several stay open till 11pm at weekends. Major museums are open every day from 10am to 7pm, and some have extended hours on Friday nights until 9pm. Many of the smaller museums are shut on Mondays.

COVID-19 Increased rates of infection may result in temporary opening hours and/or closures. Always check ahead before visiting museums, attractions and hospitality venues.

Visitor Information

The Singapore Tourism Board's information-packed Visit Singapore website *(see p111)* is constantly updated with new events.

Services offered by the main **Singapore Visitor Centre** include the sale of tours, tickets for attractions and events, and Singapore Tourist Passes. The **Chinatown Visitor Centre** offers useful information and walking tours. Hotels provide free maps of the city. These can also be picked up on arrival at Changi Airport.

Available for free at some malls, cafés, and bars, the *SG* magazine has reviews of the latest eating, shopping, and entertainment venues.

Other useful websites include **SethLui.com** for restaurant reviews, and **City Nomads** for news of the latest events, places to eat, hotels, and shops.

CityTours and **DuckTours** run hop-on, hop-off tours in open-top double-decker buses that operate along several routes and serve popular destinations in the center. **Trishaw Uncle** offers 30-minute cycle rickshaw tours around the Singapore River and Little India.

The Original Singapore Walks conduct themed walking tours through various neighborhoods with expert guides who give details about local customs, history, and heritage. They run most days except Sundays and public holidays. No reservations are required – just show up and pay the tour guide.

Local Customs

Never touch a person or even a child's head as the head is thought of as sacred in Buddhist culture. The foot is considered the lowest part of the body, and is thought to be unclean. The foot should never be used to point at someone, and you should never show the bottom of your feet. Public displays of affection should be avoided.

Language

The national language of Singapore is Malay. English, Mandarin Chinese, and Tamil are also widely spoken, with English being the most commonly used language. Visitors will also hear Singlish, a colloquial form of English spoken with a distinct accent, especially popular among younger generations.

Taxes and Refunds

Tourists who make a purchase of more than S$100 (including GST) at participating shops may claim a refund on the 8 percent Goods and Services Tax (GST) paid on their purchases. Look for a Tax Free shopping logo. Upon purchase, ask for a GST Refund form. Present the form with your receipt and the goods purchased at GST refund desks at your point of departure.

Accommodation

Singapore has a range of accommodation to suit every pocket. Super-luxury hotels can be found throughout, and especially on Sentosa, while major international chains and sleek business hotels are concentrated in the central city and financial districts, and along Orchard Road. A wide number of operators have serviced apartments for long-term guests. Boutique hotels, which often occupy heritage buildings, can be great value. Most economical hostels are found in Little India, Chinatown, and Kampong Glam. Although budget travelers will find that rooms are not as cheap as in the rest of Asia, the standards of cleanliness and amenities are high. Because Singapore is so compact, wherever you stay will feel fairly central.

As Singapore hosts business events and conventions year-round, there is no "peak season". Note that most hotels and hostels adjust their pricing depending on how full they are. Top rates apply around Christmas, and rates also increase during major sporting events or trade conventions.

DIRECTORY

CELL PHONES AND WI-FI

M1
w m1.com.sg

SingTel
w singtel.com

StarHub
w starhub.com

POSTAL SERVICES

SingPost
w singpost.com

VISITOR INFORMATION

Chinatown Visitor Centre
Kreta Ayer Square
w chinatown.sg

City Nomads
w citynomads.com/singapore

City Tours
w citytours.sg

DuckTours
w ducktours.com.sg

SethLui.com
w sethlui.com

SG
w sgmagazine.com

Singapore Visitor Centre
216 Orchard Road
t 6736-2000

The Original Singapore Walks
w journeys.com.sg/tosw

Trishaw Uncle
w trishawuncle.com.sg

Places to Stay

PRICE CATEGORIES
For a standard double room per night (with breakfast
if included), taxes and extra charges.

$ under S$200 $$ S$200–400 $$$ over S$400

Luxury Hotels

Shangri-La Hotel
MAP A3 ■ 22 Orange Grove
Rd ■ 6737-3644 ■ www.
shangri-la.com ■ $$
With 15 acres (6 ha) of
sprawling gardens, the
Shangri-La is an oasis
in the city. Guests can
choose from three styles
of accommodation: the
classically elegant rooms
of the Valley Wing, the
urban resort feel of the
Garden Wing, or the
stylish, contemporary
rooms in the Tower Wing.

Capella Singapore
MAP S3 ■ 1 The Knolls,
Sentosa ■ 6377-8888
■ www.capellahotels.
com/singapore ■ $$$
Combining restored
heritage architecture
and modern resort-style
rooms, the Capella
Singapore offers an
award-winning spa and
can arrange tours or sailing trips. The swimming
pool is beautiful, and the
elevated views are sublime.

Fairmont Singapore
MAP M1 ■ 80 Bras Basah
Rd ■ 6339-7777 ■ www.
fairmont.com/singapore
■ $$$
Each of the Fairmont's
769 luxuriously appointed
rooms and suites is its
own private sanctuary.
The hotel offers a wealth
of facilities and world-
class pampering expe-
riences, including an
award-winning spa.

Four Seasons Hotel
MAP A4 ■ 190 Orchard
Boulevard ■ 6734-1110
■ www.fourseasons.com
■ $$$
This 20-story building
is just a jog away from
the Botanic Gardens.
Rooms have charming
continental decor and
comfortable beds. The
One-Ninety restaurant
does a great Sunday
Champagne lunch.

Fullerton Hotel
MAP M3 ■ 1 Fullerton
Square ■ 6733-8388
■ www.fullertonhotels.
com ■ $$$
Converted from the
former General Post
Office, this gracious
landmark has guest
rooms with high ceilings
and long windows.
The views are spec-
tacular, overlooking
the Civic District or
Marina Bay, depend-
ing on your room.

Goodwood Park Hotel
MAP B3 ■ 22 Scotts Rd
■ 6737-7411 ■ www.
goodwoodparkhotel.com
■ $$
Built in 1900 as a club
for German expatriates,
Goodwood Park was
converted into a hotel
in 1929. The hotel
tower is a national
monument. Rooms are
classic in decor, with
contemporary amenities.
The dining options
are excellent.

Mandarin Oriental
MAP N2 ■ 5 Raffles Ave
■ 6338-0066 ■ www.
mandarin oriental.com
■ $$$
The slick and polished
Mandarin has a black
marble lobby and classic
Asian art and furnishings.
It is close to conference
venues and the Central
Business District.

Raffles Hotel
MAP M1 ■ 1 Beach Rd
■ 6337-1886 ■ www.
rafflessingapore.com
■ $$$
Opened in 1887, Raffles
features period architec-
ture and decor. All rooms
are suites with a cozy
vintage feel, and are
attended to by a butler.
Award-winning dining
options add to its appeal.

Ritz-Carlton, Millenia Singapore
MAP P2 ■ 7 Raffles Ave
■ 6337-8888 ■ www.
ritzcarlton.com ■ $$$
Located near convention
facilities and the Central
Business District, this
hotel is typically booked
by high-profile business
travelers. Contempo-
rary art pieces grace
public areas and rooms.
Marble bathrooms have
huge tubs and pano-
ramic views.

Sofitel Sentosa Resort & Spa
MAP S3 ■ 2 Bukit Manis
Rd ■ 6708-8310 ■ www.
sofitel-singapore-
sentosa.com ■ $$$
Home to Sofitel Spa,
this French-inspired
resort is set amid
lush greenery and
tropical fish ponds.

Ideal both for couples and families, most rooms promise a garden view. The Cliff restaurant has superb Italian cuisine.

The St. Regis Singapore
MAP S3 ∎ 29 Tanglin Rd ∎ 6506-6888 ∎ www.stregis.com/singapore ∎ $$$

The exclusive St. Regis is famous for its superb butler service. The truly luxurious guest rooms and suites have beautiful hand-painted silk wall coverings, designer upholstery, and French marble bathrooms. Facilities include the award-winning Remede spa, a state-of-the-art fitness center, and an outdoor spa pool.

Boutique Hotels

Amoy
MAP L4 ∎ 76 Telok Ayer St ∎ 6580-2888 ∎ www.stayfareast.com ∎ $$
Few hotels are able to have a building such as the Fuk Tak Chi museum as an entrance. This clever converted shophouse incorporates the museum as well as a warren of 37 rooms, some with suitably decorative Chinese motifs.

Ann Siang House
MAP K4 ∎ 28 Ann Siang Rd ∎ 6202-9377 ∎ www.oakwood.com ∎ $$
The 19-rooms in this hotel are intermingled with two restaurants, a basement lounge and a rooftop bar. Rooms have spacious bathrooms and luxurious furnishings and bedding, as well as exclusive toiletries.

All suites have large balconies overlooking the street below.

Hotel 1929
MAP J4 ∎ 50 Keong Saik Rd ∎ 6226-8929 ∎ www.hotel1929.com ∎ $$
Contemporary chic design is used to maximize space and brighten up this little hotel in a renovated shophouse located in the heart of Chinatown. Rooms are small.

The Vagabond Club
MAP G3 ∎ 39 Syed Alwi Rd ∎ 6291-6677 ∎ www.hotelvagabondsingapore.com ∎ $$
High-concept boutique hotel with rooms that are quirky, vibrant, and chic. Some of the boudoirs have terraces, and the restaurant and bar are acclaimed. Keep an eye out for the giant brass rhino and elephant.

Link Hotel
MAP T3 ∎ 50 Tiong Bahru Rd ∎ 6622 0505 ∎ www.linkhotel.com.sg ∎ $$
This unique Art Deco property is housed in converted apartment blocks created by an early public housing project. Located in a charming old suburb not far from Chinatown, the hotel has contemporary interiors and family rooms.

Naumi Hotel
MAP G6 ∎ 41 Seah St ∎ 6403-6000 ∎ www.naumihotel.com ∎ $$
A stylish property that is part business hotel and part boutique hotel, as it is smaller and more intimate than most. Rooms and facilities

at the Naumi focus on state-of-the-art technology and edgy design.

The Scarlet Hotel
MAP K5 ∎ 33 Erskine Rd ∎ 6511-3333 ∎ www.thescarletsingapore.com ∎ $$
An experience for the senses, the Scarlet Hotel is swathed in deep velvet, silk, and satin, with bespoke furnishings and glistening lacquer accents. The suites are cozy and intimate, but the standard and deluxe rooms are tiny, so it may not be ideal for those staying more than a few days.

Business Hotels

PARKROYAL COLLECTION Pickering
MAP K3 ∎ 33 Upper Pickering St ∎ 6809-8888 ∎ www.panpacific.com ∎ $$
Close to the Central Business District, this eco-conscious hotel features large work spaces in its guest rooms, including lushly planted terraces and sky gardens.

Crowne Plaza Changi Airport
MAP V2 ∎ 75 Airport Boulevard ∎ 6823-5300 ∎ www.changiairport.crowneplaza.com ∎ $$
Crowne Plaza was Singapore's first international business hotel to be located at the airport. The location is still close enough for quick trips into town. The hotel is also close to the Singapore EXPO and the East Coast industrial parks.

InterContinental
MAP G5 ▪ 80 Middle Rd ▪ 6338-7600 ▪ www. singaporeintercontinental. com ▪ $$
Built atop a cluster of pre-war shophouses, the hotel has absorbed these original structures as well as local style into its decor. It is located above an MRT station not far from the Suntec Convention Center.

M Hotel
MAP K6 ▪ 81 Anson Rd ▪ 6224-1133 ▪ www. m-hotel.com ▪ $$
Located inside the Shenton Way financial district, this business hotel offers top-class facilities, including multiple dining options, a robotic breakfast chef, as well as a business center and office suites on level 8. Weekend guests can enjoy some good discounts.

PARKROYAL COLLECTION Marina Bay
MAP N2 ▪ 6 Raffles Boulevard ▪ 6845-1000 ▪ www.panpacific.com ▪ $$
Built around an atrium lobby, this business hotel is connected to the Marina Square shopping mall. The views from the rooms that face the bay are terrific.

Sheraton Towers
MAP C2 ▪ 39 Scotts Rd ▪ 6737-6888 ▪ www. sheratonsingapore.com ▪ $$
Centrally located, this 420-room hotel is known for its outstanding quality and great service. Equipped with modern amenities and conveniences, the hotel's

elegant rooms offer contemporary comfort and stylish sophistication.

Conrad Centennial
MAP N2 ▪ 2 Temasek Boulevard ▪ 6334-8888 ▪ www.hilton.com/en/ conrad ▪ $$$
Guest rooms at the hotel are located in two towers and feature state-of-the-art communications facilities. It also has conference rooms, a business center a swimming pool and multiple dining options.

Grand Hyatt
MAP B4 ▪ 10 Scotts Rd ▪ 6738-1234 ▪ www. singapore.grand.hyatt. com ▪ $$$
The check-in area here is located out of view of the main doors. While the Grand Rooms are larger, the Terrace Wing rooms have bright workspaces. Some suites feature a study or a meeting area.

Marina Bay Sands
MAP N4 ▪ 10 Bayfront Ave ▪ 6688-8888 ▪ www. marinabaysands.com ▪ $$$
The leading resort destination in Asia, this hotel features convention and exhibition facilities, 2,560 rooms and suites, two theaters, the rooftop Sands SkyPark, and world-class restaurants. Completing the line-up of attractions is the ArtScience Museum at Marina Bay Sands.

JW Marriott Singapore South Beach
MAP N2 ▪ 30 Beach Rd ▪ 6818-1888 ▪ www. marriott.com ▪ $$$
The South Beach has splendid views and is

across the road from Suntec City. Rooms are designed by Philippe Starck, plus there are two outdoor infinity pools and super chic dining.

Singapore Marriott Tang Plaza Hotel
MAP B4 ▪ 320 Orchard Rd ▪ 6735-5800 ▪ www. marriott.com ▪ $$$
Located in the heart of the city's business, shopping, and entertainment district, the Singapore Marriott offers both business and leisure travelers the highest level of luxury.

Family Hotels

YMCA@One Orchard
MAP E6 ▪ 1 Orchard Rd ▪ 6336-6000 ▪ www.ymca ih.com.sg ▪ $
Of the several YMCAs in Singapore, this one is hard to beat for location – just a couple of minutes' walk from the National Museum and other historic sights as well as bustling Orchard Road. It also has a café, a pool, and a gym. The rooms here include family rooms and junior suites.

YWCA Fort Canning Lodge
MAP E6 ▪ 6 Fort Canning Rd ▪ 6338-4222 ▪ www. ywcafortcanning.org.sg ▪ $
Like the YMCA close by, the YWCA enjoys a central location. The refurbished rooms and family suites are a good size with views of the pool or the park. There is a café that is open all day and a self-service laundry; the staff are friendly and helpful.

Holiday Inn Singapore Orchard City Centre

MAP D5 ▪ 11 Cavenagh Rd ▪ 6733-8333 ▪ www.ihg.com/holidayinn ▪ $$

This hotel has rooms that are large, clean, and well-equipped with fridges and coffee-making facilities. There is a decent breakfast buffet, service standards are high, and there is a rooftop pool and a fitness center. Two restaurants, Tandoor and Window on the Park, and a bar complete the package.

Orchard Rendezvous Hotel

MAP A4 ▪ 1 Tanglin Rd ▪ 6737-1133 ▪ www.rendezvoushotels.com.sg ▪ $$

The location is great for such a good price. This hotel has a lovely pool, good laundry facilities, and family studios with lounge and dining areas.

PARKROYAL on Beach Road

MAP H5 ▪ 7500 Beach Rd ▪ 6505-5666 ▪ www.panpacific.com ▪ $$

Close to Arab Street, the PARKROYAL has good facilities at a reasonable price. There are inter-connecting rooms for families, and activities for children. The rooftop pool is popular with kids.

Siloso Beach Resort

MAP S3 ▪ 51 Imbiah Walk, Sentosa ▪ 6722-3333 ▪ www.siloso beachresort.com ▪ $$

The glass walls of this resort offer great views of the beach, and it is just a short walk to the sea. There are one- and two-bedroom villas, as well

as the rooms in the main hotel. The leisure facilities are excellent, and there is a waterfall pool.

Village Hotel Bugis

MAP G5 ▪ 390 Victoria St ▪ 6297-2828 ▪ www.villagehotels.asia ▪ $$

A bustling hotel that is family-friendly to the extent that it even has themed rooms for kids, with child-friendly toiletries and cartoon wallpaper. It is centrally located on the edge of Kampong Glam.

JEN Singapore Tanglin

MAP A4 ▪ 1A Cuscaden Rd ▪ 6738-2222 ▪ www.shangri-la.com/hotels/jen ▪ $$

A 10-minute walk from the Botanic Garden, this stylish hotel offers discounts on family accommodation. The rooftop swimming pool comes complete with colorful floats.

Festive Hotel

MAP S3 ▪ Resorts World Sentosa ▪ 6577-8899 ▪ www.rwsentosa.com ▪ $$$

Catering to children just as much as adults, this hotel offers fun welcome packs and candy at reception and specially tailored bathrobes for kids. The deluxe family rooms are separated into two areas with a king-sized bed for parents and a loft bed that youngsters will love.

Fraser Place

MAP J2 ▪ 11 Unity St ▪ 6736-4800 ▪ www.frasershospitality.com ▪ $$$

For stays of more than a week, Fraser Place has well-equipped one-,

two-, and three-bedroom apartments right on the riverfront. There is a playground and a pool with a supermarket and cafés nearby.

Shangri-La Rasa Sentosa

MAP S3 ▪ 101 Siloso Rd ▪ 6371-1088 ▪ www.shangri-la.com ▪ $$$

The only beachfront hotel in Singapore is an attractive choice for families. The children's club features a tree-house slide and a range of organized activities. There is also a children's pool, with water slides. All rooms have a balcony overlooking the hills or the South China Sea.

Value-for-Money Hotels

Hotel Bencoolen

MAP F5 ▪ 47 Bencoolen St ▪ 6460-4933 ▪ www.hotelbencoolen.com ▪ $

Only a few minutes' walk away from Orchard Road and Little India, the Bencoolen's location makes it a good choice. The rooms are clean and equipped with TVs and coffee-making facilities. Breakfast is a Western style buffet, and there is a modest rooftop pool.

Hotel Re!

MAP J4 ▪ 175A Chin Swee Rd ▪ 6827 8288 ▪ www.hotelre.com.sg ▪ $

The retro furnishings and psychedelic decor (including glittery mosaic bath tiles) of this hotel attract a younger clientele. Located only a 15-minute walk from Chinatown and with friendly staff, the Hotel Re! is a good-value option.

For a key to hotel price categories see p114

Hotel Yan

MAP H2 ■ 162 Tyrwhitt Rd ■ 6805-1955 ■ www.hotel-yan.com ■ $

Backpackers can up the budget a bit to enjoy industrial-chic in this cozy hotel not far from Little India and Kampong Glam. Rooms here are small but well equipped, with picture windows and complimentary snacks and toiletries.

The Inn at Temple Street

MAP K4 ■ 36 Temple St ■ 6221-5333 ■ www.theinn.com.sg ■ $

Right in the heart of the Chinatown Conservation Area, this award-winning inn takes up a row of five renovated shophouses. It is not strong on modern comforts and the rooms are small, but it has a charm that is unusual at this price.

Keong Saik Hotel

MAP J4 ■ 69 Keong Saik Rd ■ 6223-0660 ■ www.keongsaikhotel.com.sg ■ $

One of several Singapore hotels set in converted shophouses, Keong Saik has small, sparsely furnished rooms. Though modest, they are clean, and decorative molding surrounds windows overlooking an attractive Chinatown lane.

Hotel Clover The Arts

MAP L3 ■ 58 South Bridge Rd ■ 6439-7088 ■ www.thearts.hotelclover.com ■ $

Many of the cozy, well-equipped rooms at this quirky hotel feature murals by local design students. Boat Quay and the river are less than a 10-minute walk away.

Perak Hotel

MAP F4 ■ 12 Perak Rd ■ 6299-7733 ■ www.theperakhotel.com ■ $

The friendly front-desk staff make guests feel at home in this small guesthouse in Little India. It has comfortable rooms, with dressing tables, closets, and en suite bathrooms. An unfussy café serves free breakfast for guests.

Heritage Collection on Seah

MAP M1 ■ 39 Seah St ■ 6223-7155 ■ www.hericoll.com ■ $

Within walking distance of the museums, this Civic District hotel is housed in a renovated shophouse. It has compact, split-level studios neatly designed to include a work space and a kitchenette. The building also has shared laundry facilities. It is a great option for solo travelers.

Strand Hotel

MAP F5 ■ 25 Bencoolen St ■ 6338-1866 ■ www.strandhotel.com.sg ■ $

Located close to Orchard Road, the Strand does not look like a budget place. Rooms are large and colorful with a range of deluxe and family rooms, which can accommodate up to five guests, and the staff is friendly.

Summer View Hotel

MAP F5 ■ 173 Bencoolen St ■ 6338-1122 ■ www.summerviewhotel.com.sg ■ $

This inexpensive hotel is surrounded by a host of attractions. It has all the basics – breakfast buffet, cable TV, Internet, and coffee-making facilities, but no pool.

Albert Court Village Hotel

MAP F4 ■ 180 Albert St ■ 6339-3939 ■ www.villagehotels.asia ■ $$

This lovely little hotel is decorated with Peranakan textiles, carved wood furnishings, and traditional floral tiles. There is a gym, Jacuzzis, and a coffee shop, while the central courtyard is a popular place to hang out.

Hotel Grand Central

MAP D5 ■ 22 Cavenagh Rd ■ 6737-9944 ■ www.grandcentral.com.sg ■ $

Offering a great location at a good price, this 1970s hotel does not offer much in the way of facilities. However, it may appeal to visitors who use a hotel as a crash pad and want to be close to Orchard Road.

Lloyd's Inn

MAP J1 ■ 2 Lloyd Rd ■ 6737-7309 ■ www.lloydsinn.com ■ $

An intimate, sociable hotel with an excellent location near Orchard Road. The roof terrace is lovely, and minimalist design throughout makes the most of light and air. Although facilities are limited, it also includes a dipping pool surrounded with lush foliage.

M Social

MAP T3 ■ 90 Robertson Quay ■ 6206-1888 ■ www.millenniumhotels.com ■ $$

Trendy and techy, this hotel sports cutting-edge design by Philippe Starck, with contrasting textiles and tiles. The social aspect is played out through open communal spaces for visitors to interact. It also has an Asian-fusion resto-bar,

Beasts & Butterflies, a fitness center, and quirky yet sophisticated rooms.

Peninsula Excelsior Hotel

MAP L2 ▪ 5 Coleman St ▪ 6337-2200 ▪ www. peninsulaexcelsior.com. sg ▪ $$

The result of a merger of the Excelsior and Peninsula hotels gives you twice the facilities and two pools. Ask for a room facing Marina Bay – you will not get a better view at the price.

RELC International Hotel

MAP A2 ▪ 30 Orange Grove Rd ▪ 6885-7888 ▪ www.relcih.com.sg ▪ $

RELC offers an excellent combination of location and facilities at a very good price. There is a decent range of rooms and prices, but all are reasonably large and equipped with balconies, cable TV, fridge, and coffee-making facilities. The free breakfast isn't brilliant, but there are plenty of tempting options on Orchard Road, just 10 minutes' walk away.

Hostels and Guesthouses

Adler Hostel

MAP K4 ▪ 259 South Bridge Rd ▪ 6226-0173 ▪ www.adlerhostel.com ▪ $

A charming hostel that looks fancy enough to be mistaken for a furniture store from the outside, this hostel has "cabins" for beds – posh pod-style affairs. There is an indoor garden and a small café as well.

Wink Chinatown

MAP K4 ▪ 8A Mosque St ▪ 9835-6850 ▪ www. winkhostel.com ▪ $

Located in Chinatown, this modern hostel has air-conditioned rooms with custom-made pods to sleep in. Facilities include Wi-Fi, laundry service, and a kitchenette. It also offers complimentary breakfast.

Beary Best! Hostel

MAP K4 ▪ 16 Upper Cross St ▪ 6222-4957 ▪ www. bearybesthostel.com ▪ $

This hostel in Chinatown provides a cozy ambience and useful facilities. It is also great value for money, with a location that is just a few steps away from Chinatown MRT station.

Betel Box

MAP T2 ▪ 200 Joo Chiat Rd ▪ 6247-7340 ▪ www. betelbox.com ▪ $

The modern Asian decor here reflects the building's heritage as a former shophouse. The Joo Chiat area where it is located is home to a number of restaurants. It also organizes tours of interesting neighborhoods, both old and new.

Cube@Kampong Glam

MAP H5 ▪ 55 Bussorah St ▪ 6291-1696 ▪ www. cubehotels.com.sg/ kampong-glam ▪ $

Located in Kampong Glam, this charming, plush hostel offers dorms that have capsule beds, built-in safes, charging points and reading lights. There's a cozy breakfast area at the back.

Dream Lodge

MAP H2 ▪ 172 Tyrwhitt Rd ▪ 6816-1036 ▪ www. dreamlodge.sg ▪ $

Designed for those looking to interact with other travelers, this community lodge has pod-style beds, some suitable for couples, and a pleasant lounge. There are a few quirky cafés and bars within walking distance.

The Hive Backpackers' Hostel

MAP G2 ▪ 624 Serangoon Rd ▪ 8168-4337 ▪ www. the-hive-hostel.business. site ▪ $

Not quite centrally located, but clean and safe, this hostel has private rooms – some en suite – and dorms, which are all air-conditioned. Breakfast is included, and a lounge offers cable TV.

The InnCrowd Backpackers' Hostel

MAP F4 ▪ 73 Dunlop St ▪ 6296-9169 ▪ www. the-inncrowd.com ▪ $

A well-planned place, this spacious Little India hostel is one of the cheapest in Singapore. All air-conditioned dormitories and private rooms have access to bathrooms, a kitchenette, an on-site pub serving cheap beer, a travel library, as well as a rooftop sundeck.

Met A Space Pod

MAP L3 ▪ 51A Boat Quay ▪ 6635-2694 ▪ www.meta spacepod.com.sg ▪ $

This hostel has high-tech, capsule-style beds which give you the feeling of sleeping inside your own cylinder within a space probe. The kitchen, bathrooms and breakfasts are much more down-to-earth.

General Index

Acknowledgments

This edition updated by

Contributor M. Astella Saw
Senior Editor Alison McGill
Senior Designer Stuti Tiwari Bhatia
Project Editors Dipika Dasgupta,
Rada Radojicic
Editor Anuroop Sanwalia
Assistant Editor Anjasi Nongkynrih
Nyshadham
Picture Research Administrator
Vagisha Pushp
Publishing Assistant Halima Mohammed
Picture Research Manager Taiyaba Khatoon
Jacket Designer Jordan Lambley
Senior Cartographer Subhashree Bharati
Cartography Manager Suresh Kumar
DTP Designer Rohit Rojal
Senior Production Editor Jason Little
Production Controller Samantha Cross
Deputy Managing Editor Beverly Smart
Managing Editors Shikha Kulkarni,
Hollie Teaque
Managing Art Editor Sarah Snelling
Senior Managing Art Editor Priyanka Thakur
Art Director Maxine Pedliham
Publishing Director Georgina Dee

DK would like to thank the following for
their contribution to the previous editions:
Susy Atkinson, Vanessa Betts, Jennifer
Eveland, Richard Lim, Clare Peel, Helen Peters

The publisher would like to thank the
following for their kind permission to
reproduce their photographs:
Key: a-above; b-below/bottom; c-center;
t-far; l-left; r-right; t-top

123RF.com: Pisit Khambubpha 83b; saiko3p
71b; Ignasi Such 73cl.

Acid Bar: 56c.

Alamy Stock Photo: Stephen Belcher 79tr;
dbimages / Betty Johnson 45cl; Chronicle
36tr, Paul Dymond 26cr, Granger - Historical
Picture Archive, Nyc 36b; imageBROKER /
Peter Schickert 22-3, / Valentin Wolf 2tl, 8-9;
John Warburton Lee Photography / Andrew
Watson 4cr; JTB Media Creation, Inc. 85cla;
Jason Knott 27tl; Jon Lord 97cl;
NiceProspects-Singapore 18cla; Sean Pavone
4b; pbpvision 21br; Simon Reddy 74tr;
REUTERS / Roger Bacon 67cla; Prasit
Rudphan 20-?, Peter Schickert 4t; Fedor
Selivanov 80c; Lee Snider 16br; Antony Souter
17tl, 17br, 19br, 76tc, Stock Connection Blue /
Dallas and John Heaton 4clb; Simon Reddy
105cra; Steve Vidler 61cla; Maximilian
Weinzierl 32-3.

Asian Civilisations Museum: 14clb, 41c, 43br.

Bugis+: 92b.

Chinatown Heritage Centre: Victor Chick Wh
40br, 71tr.

Dreamstime.com: Ahau1969 25cr; Ahxiong
88tl; Ake1150sb 6br; Arndale 4cla; Boggy
70tl; Chingyunsong 43cra; Cristinnastoian
11tr; Kobby Dagan 20br; Dolphfyn 61tr;
Eugenelow 90b; Evolution1088 51tr, 94c;
F11photo 26-27ca; Gianguyen189 89b;
Gnohz 4cl; Renan Greinert 20cl; Haslinda
24bl; Iorboaz 10bl, 80tl; Irishka777 11cr;
Irynarasko 30-1; Jimmytst 46tr, 62cla;
Jirousek 101tl; Joshelerry 27br; Jpldesigns
65cl; Kheng1987 25tl; Korkorkorpai 11clb;
Kuba 101br; Leungchopan 14-5; Louisescott
21crb; Minyun9260 24-5, 96c; Luciano
Mortula 7clb; Mvtmdn 25bc; Naruto4836
63tl; Platongkoh 28crb; Potongsaga 59cb;
Presse750 31tl; Prestonia 12cla; Quanstills
38b; Ravijohnsmith 10cl; Ronniechua 20-1;
Saiko3p 15bl; Salparadis 47c; Samanthatan
44b; Schlenger86 100cla; Sepavo 4crb;
Siblingstudio 74c; Ravindran Smith 63br;
Sosharp 2tr, 34-5; Pu Sulan 26bl; Wai
Chung Tung 91cl; Tang90246 44tl, 65br,
Themorningglory 3tl, 68-9; Tktktk 6cla;
Tomas1111 11ca; Tongtranson 7tr, 66b;
Toomtamgeo 46-7; Dongli Zhang 89tl.

FLPA: ImageBroker 24cb.

Getty Images: AFP / Roslan Rahman 67br, /
Roslan Rahman 96tl; Arterra / UIG 72br;
Atlantide Phototravel 62br; Gonzalo Azumendi
19tl, 81bl; Allan Baxter 10crb; Bloomberg /
Nicky Loh 40cla; John Seaton Callahan 3tr,
106-7; Wendy Chan 75cla; EyeEm / Chee Hoe
Fong 66tc; EyeEm / Fumiko Mizuno 104clb;
fiftymm99 50b, 66cla; Manfred Gottschalk
16-7; Dave and Les Jacobs 39tr; Jean-Pierre
Lescourret 95tl; MediaNews Group / Orange
County Register / Kevin Sullivan 37tr; Calvin
Chan Wai Meng 72t; Thomas Müller 42t;
Poppertoto / Paul Popper 37cl, 45tr;
robertharding / Amanda Hall 10cb; Baerbel
Schmidt 40tl, simonlong 79br; siwarock 102c;
Chan Srithaweeporn 64t; ullstein bild /
Dagmar Scherf 84bl.

Goodwood Park Hotel: 96b.

Harry's International-Boat Quay. 57cl.

Invade Industry PTE LTD: 51cl.

iStockphoto.com: Roman Babakin 54-5;
poludziber 86-87.

Mandarin Oriental: 49t.

Marina Bay Sands Pte Ltd: Rory Daniel 56t;
Eyeamseeingthings / Koh Sze Kiat 28bl.

National Gallery Singapore: 55cr.

National Heritage Board, Singapore:
Collection of Indian Heritage Centre 82cb.

**Courtesy of National Museum of Singapore,
National Heritage Board:** 10ca, 12bl, 12cb,
13tl, 13crb, 41t.

NParks: 103cl.

NUS Museum: 54tl.

Potato Head Folk Theatre: 77cr.

Raffles Hotel/FRHI Hotels & Resorts: 30ca, 30bl, 31tl, 31bl, 31crb.

Resorts World Sentosa: 11br, 32bl, 33crb, 33bl, 53bl.

The Ritz-Carlton, Millenia Sinagpore: 59t.

Robert Harding Picture Library: Fraser Hall 1, Christian Kober 16cla.

Shanghai Tang: martinstudio 98t.

Shangri-La Hotel, Singapore: 99clb.

Shutterstock: DerekTeo 90tl; EQRoy 52cb; Hafiz Bin Ismail 53tr; Dr David Sing 60b; Danny Ye 15crb.

Sofitel Singapore Sentosa Resort & Spa: 48tc.

Spa Esprit Dempsey: 48br.

Sultan Mosque: 18crb.

Sun Yat Sen Nanyang Memorial Hall: National Heritage Board Singapore 102t.

TINTIN SINGAPORE PTE LTD: 76cl

The White Rabbit/ The Lo & Behold Group: 58br.

Wild Wild Wet - NTUC Club: 52tl.

Wolfgang Puck Fine Dining Group: 93crb

Cover

Front and spine: **Robert Harding Picture Library:** Fraser Hall.

Back: **Alamy Stock Photo:** Horizon Images / Motion crb, icpix_singapore cl; Roland Nagy tl, Prasit Rodphan tr; **Robert Harding Picture Library:** Fraser Hall b.

Pull Out Map Cover

Robert Harding Picture Library: Fraser Hal.

All other images © Dorling Kindersley
For further information see:
www.dkimages.com

DK | Penguin Random House

First Edition 2009

Published in Great Britain by
Dorling Kindersley Limited
DK, One Embassy Gardens, 8 Viaduct
Gardens, London SW11 7BW, UK

The authorised representative in the EEA is
Dorling Kindersley Verlag GmbH. Arnulfstr.
124, 80636 Munich, Germany

Published in the United States by
DK Publishing, 1745 Broadway, 20th Floor,
New York, NY 10019, USA

Copyright © 2009, 2022 Dorling
Kindersley Limited
A Penguin Random House Company

22 23 24 25 10 9 8 7 6 5 4 3 2 1

A CIP catalog record is available
from the British Library.

A catalog record for this book is available
from the Library of Congress.

ISSN 1479-344X

ISBN 978-0-2415-6892-7

Printed and bound in Malaysia

www.dk.com

As a guide to abbreviations in visitor information blocks: **Adm** *= admission charge;* **D** *= dinner.*

MIX
Paper from
responsible sources
FSC™ C018179
www.fsc.org